POETRY SOCIETY OF AMERICA
ANTHOLOGY

EDITED BY

**Amy Bonner, Melville Cane,
Gwendolen Haste, Alfred Kreymborg
Leonora Speyer, A. M. Sullivan**

THE
Poetry Society of America
ANTHOLOGY

INTRODUCTION BY J. DONALD ADAMS

Granger Index Reprint Series

BOOKS FOR LIBRARIES PRESS
FREEPORT, NEW YORK

Publisher's Note

IN SELECTING POEMS for this Anthology, the editors
limited themselves to the consideration of member
poets (past and present) whose work was available
for use; and in order to keep the book within sizable
bounds, the editors further limited themselves to the
acceptance of a maximum of three poems from each
living contributor and one from each deceased member.
The decision to restrict representation of deceased members to one poem each was made for the purpose of giving
preponderance to living members.

The absence from the Anthology of the work of a
number of member poets is attributable to (1) failure
on the part of these members to submit poems for consideration and (2) failure to submit poems which, in
the judgment of the editors, were deemed worthy of
inclusion.

The single poem by which deceased members are
represented is not invariably the one by which they are
best known. The editors sought, wherever possible, to
avoid duplication of poems found in other anthologies
and to offer, instead, poems not so generally known yet
representative.

The publisher wishes to thank all those who contributed their time and labor in the compilation of the
Anthology, particularly the original publishers and
copyright owners who, in view of the non-profit nature

v

of the venture, very generously waived reprint fees; to the members of the editorial board for a difficult task well done; to Jessie B. Rittenhouse, whose first-hand knowledge of the early history of the society and familiarity with the work of past members proved invaluable to the editors; to Starr Nelson for her help in the preparation of the biographical notes; and to all members of the society who submitted their poems for consideration and made this Anthology possible.

Introduction

THE FIRST MEETING of The Poetry Society of America was held in New York at the National Arts Club in October, 1910. Thus it is evident that the founding of the Society preceded by just a little that extraordinary revival of interest in poetry which, in England, is commonly dated from the publication of Masefield's *The Everlasting Mercy* in 1911, and in America, from the founding of *Poetry: A Magazine of Verse,* in 1912.

In that revival the Poetry Society played a leading part. It provided poetry with a forum in which the new developments were excitedly—and excitingly—discussed. No political meetings were more turbulent than some of the sessions of the Poetry Society during the years when the renascence was at its height. There can be no doubt, I think, that poetry was the better for the Society's existence; its effect was vitalizing and encouraging. It was typical of the public neglect into which poetry had fallen, that when the Pulitzer prizes were established, no provision was made for the poetry award. Through the efforts of Edward J. Wheeler, the first president of the Society, funds were obtained and accepted by Columbia University; a few years later, as a direct result of the Society's sponsorship, the original provisions of the Pulitzer bequest were enlarged to ensure the continuance of the award.

When poetry began to lose once more the larger audience that had been won back for it, the Society steadfastly continued its work. Through its influence, local replicas of the parent society were being organized all over the country, and today, from coast to coast, these State societies foster interest in poetry and give an encouragement to many lovers of the art, that would otherwise be lacking.

It seemed fitting, in view of the Society's history, its services to poetry, the long roster of distinguished names in its membership, that it should have its own anthology. The editors faced a task of exceptional difficulty; I think they are to be congratulated on the good sense and sound taste with which they have performed it. The membership of the Society, living and dead, includes some of the great names in the history of American poetry, and a very impressive collection could of course have been made from the work of these alone. But it was the aim of the editors to build their selections upon as broad a base as possible, to reflect as well as they could the wide range of talents which the Society's membership has contained from its beginning. Some of the most famous names in American poetry are represented here by but a single poem, and there are remarkably fine poems under names that are hardly known to the reading public. There are more than two hundred poets represented, ranging from the acknowledged great to the obscure, but every reader of this anthology will be impressed, I think, by the prevailing level of distinction.

J. DONALD ADAMS

Contents

Publisher's Note   v
Introduction by J. Donald Adams   vii

MARGUERITE JANVRIN ADAMS
    Prayer in an Arctic Season   1

SARA VAN ALSTYNE ALLEN
    The Zoo in the City   1

DOROTHY ALYEA
    Portrait of Two Unhappy Young People   2

JOHN WILLIAMS ANDREWS
    New Wonder   3

MARY AUSTIN
    The Eagle's Song   4

KARLE WILSON BAKER
    I Shall Be Loved as Quiet Things   5

ELSA BARKER
    The Two Selves   6
    When I Am Dead   6

ISABEL HARRISS BARR
    Answer from Assisi   7

LAURA BENET
    Crowning   8

STEPHEN VINCENT BENET
    American Names   8

WILLIAM ROSE BENET
    Two North Shore Poems   10

GERTRUDE RYDER BENNETT
    Tropical Fish   11

JOHN PEALE BISHOP
    Encounter   12

JOHN BLACK
    Song Comes Like a Frustrated Flower   13

ELIZABETH BOHM
Tracks   14

AMY BONNER
House Long Known   15

CARL JOHN BOSTELMANN
Harper's Ferry   16

BIANCA BRADBURY
Farmer's Wife   16

ANN BRADSHAW
One Black Crow   17

ANNA HEMPSTEAD BRANCH
In the Beginning Was the Word   18

FLORENCE KERR BROWNELL
Strawberry Mark   21

NANCY BRUFF
The One Ambassador   22

ELIZABETH J. BUCHTENKIRK
Black Soldier   23

HELEN BURLIN
Caterpillar   23

STRUTHERS BURT
We Are Wonderful, We Are Wise   24

RICHARD BURTON
Black Sheep   25

FRANCES WESTGATE BUTTERFIELD
Le Printemps Empoissoné   26

WITTER BYNNER
Defeat   27

MELVILLE CANE
Behind Dark Spaces   27
Askew, We Ask You   28
Hymn to Night   29

SARA KING CARLETON
Cathedral   30

BLISS CARMAN
A Vagabond Song   31

MADISON CAWEIN
Deserted   31

KATHERINE GARRISON CHAPIN
Love Beleaguered 32

THOMAS CALDECOT CHUBB
Wild Duck Song 33

GERTRUDE CLAYTOR
Indian Wife 34

CATHERINE CATE COBLENTZ
Hakluyt and the "English Voyages" 35

STANTON A. COBLENTZ
The Woods Shall not Be Lonely 36

ROBERT P. TRISTRAM COFFIN
The Secret Heart 37

GLADYS CROMWELL
The Crowning Gift 38

HENRY DALTON
Short Story 38

EARL DANIELS
Small Apocalypse 39

GUSTAV DAVIDSON
The Golden Leopard 40
Mortal Hunger 40

MARY CAROLYN DAVIES
Hunger 41
On Becoming a Book 42

JULIA JOHNSON DAVIS
John 43
To an Ass 44

ELMER DEAN
The Stallion 44

AUGUST DERLETH
Lost Child 45
Wild Apples 46

SAMUEL A. DE WITT
Quatrains for a Bank Cashier 49

GEORGE DILLON
Address to the Doomed (I, III, IX) 49

ALLAN D. DOWLING
The Arrow's Death 51

JANE DRANSFIELD
  The Great Square   51
  Eight Doves   53

THEODORE DREISER
  Evening-Mountains   54

ESTELLE DUCLO
  O Nations!   55

MARY BALLARD DURYEE
  And the Days Were Accomplished   56

MARY CUMMINGS EUDY
  Oxen   56

ROSEMARY FARRAR
  The Cocks Have Crowed   57

ARTHUR DAVISON FICKE
  Long and Lovely   58

MAHLON LEONARD FISHER
  When I Am Ended   58

KIMBALL FLACCUS
  To Alfred Kreymborg   59

JOHN GOULD FLETCHER
  Renewal Time   61

RALPH FRIEDRICH
  Of Poems   62

ELIZABETH HOLLISTER FROST
  Dust   63

ROBERT FROST
  A Considerable Speck   64
  The Most of It   65
  Come In   65

ETHEL ROMIG FULLER
  The Dark Chamber   66

THEODOSIA GARRISON
  Stains   67

MINNA GELLERT
  Translation From a Lost Language   68
  Flesh of the Furies   68

CLIFFORD GESSLER
  Siesta Hour   69

Contents

xiii

KAHLIL GIBRAN
Love 70

YETZA GILLESPIE
Blue Heron 71

LOUIS GINSBERG
When Bombs on Barcelona Burst 72

MAE WINKLER GOODMAN
Emily Dickinson 72

WILLIAM GRIFFITH
Pierrette in Memory 73

LOUISE IMOGEN GUINEY
Irish Peasant Song 74

ARTHUR GUITERMAN
On the Vanity of Earthly Greatness 74

RALPH GUSTAFSON
On the Struma Massacre 75
Flight into Darkness 75

HERMANN HAGEDORN
Doors 77

AMANDA BENJAMIN HALL
The School Boy Learns to Fly 77
Instant out of Time 78

HAZEL HALL
Two Sewing 79

MARION ETHEL HAMILTON
Children on a Hill 80

LEIGH HANES
Screech Owls 80
Moon Magic 81

ELIZABETH STANTON HARDY
The Aristocrat 81
Signature upon Rock 82

AMORY HARE
The Crown 83

GWENDOLEN HASTE
Death of the Grandmother 83
Ophidia 85

FANNY DE GROOT HASTINGS
  Coral Lizard   86

SARA HENDERSON HAY
  The Beasts   87
  Child on the Beach   87

DANIEL HENDERSON
  Consider, Lord, our Clerk   88

DUBOSE HEYWARD
  The Mountain Woman   88

SOPHIE HIMMELL
  Sleep   89

DOROTHY HOBSON
  Awakening   90

MARCIA NICHOLS HOLDEN
  Convent   91

RAYMOND HOLDEN
  The Mind Has Studied Flight   92
  Awake under Stars   93

FRANCES MINTURN HOWARD
  Foundation   94
  Martyr   94

DOROTHY BERRY HUGHES
  The Hand   95

JOSEPHINE JACOBSEN
  For a Dancer   95
  Midnight Eden   96

LESLIE NELSON JENNINGS
  Carpentry   97

ORRICK JOHNS
  Tree Toad   97
  Wild Plum   98

JOSEPHINE JOHNSON
  Low Country   99

VICTORIA SAFFELLE JOHNSON
  The Great Blue Heron   100

LEILA JONES
  Locket for the Heart   101

MARY HOXIE JONES
  Harvest   101

RUTH LAMBERT JONES
Prevision 103

THOMAS S. JONES, JR.
Clonmacnoise 103

HANNAH KAHN
No More Poems 104

LUCY KENT
Winter Overture 105

ALINE KILMER
My Mirror 106

JOYCE KILMER
Prayer of a Soldier in France 107

SALLY BRUCE KINSOLVING
Go Down, Moses 108

FARONA KONOPAK
Largo 108

ALFRED KREYMBORG
Under Glass 109
Credo 109
Human Throne 110

FANIA KRUGER
Wandering Child 111

ALEXANDER LAING
David To day 111

GORDON LAWRENCE
Third Avenue 114
Museum Piece 114

RUTH LECHLITNER
Song of Starlings 115
Only the Years 116

RICHARD LEGALLIENNE
What of the Darkness? 117

LAURA LOURENE LEGEAR
Water Moccasin 118

MARY SINTON LEITCH
He Who Loves the Ocean 119

JESSIE LEMONT
Diana Remembers Actaeon 120

WILLIAM ELLERY LEONARD
Sonnets from "Two Lives"   121

MAY LEWIS
Days at Sea   122
The Grass   123

ELIAS LIEBERMAN
To My Brothers Everywhere   124
Sitting-Room in a Bowery Hotel   124

ANNE MORROW LINDBERGH
Elegy Under the Stars   125

VACHEL LINDSAY
Abraham Lincoln Walks at Midnight   126

CAROLYN WILSON LINK
Apology to My Heirs   127

GORDDEN LINK
The Deaf   128

SARAH LITSEY
Skunk Cabbage Rising in March   130

ANNE LLOYD
Two Powers   130

AMY LOWELL
Lilacs   131

HOLGER LUNDBERGH
When a Gull Falls   135

GERTRUDE MAY LUTZ
Golgotha   136
Concept   136

MAUREEN COBB MABBOTT
Imperious Design   137

CHRISTY MACKAYE
Speech   137

PERCY MACKAYE
My Love and I   138

SISTER M. MADELEVA
November Afternoons   140
Riddles, One, Two and Three   140

EDWIN MARKHAM
Lincoln, The Man of the People   141

LENORE G. MARSHALL
This Twentieth Century Mind 143
As Though from Love 143

GILBERT MAXWELL
"It Was Good for the Hebrew Children" 145

DAVID MCCORD
A Star by Day 146

VIRGINIA TAYLOR MCCORMICK
Apostrophe to a Fighter Plane 147

ALICE MONKS MEARS
Brief Enterprise 148
What Spirit? 148

MARJORIE MEEKER
The Magnolia Tree 149

GERARD PREVIN MEYER
There Is a Street 150

EDNA ST. VINCENT MILLAY
On Hearing a Symphony of Beethoven 151
To Jesus on His Birthday 151
The Buck in the Snow 152

JOAQUIN MILLER
Columbus 153

MARY OWINGS MILLER
Camouflage of the Willow Ptarmigan 154

VIRGINIA SCOTT MINER
Mouse in a Florist's Window 155

EDITH MIRICK
Drought 155

HARRIET MONROE
The Water Ouzel 156

VAIDA STEWART MONTGOMERY
I Am Desert-Born 157

EDWIN MORGAN
At the Shore 157

HELEN MORROW
Two Deer in a Glade 158

DAVID MORTON
Pieties (I, II) 160

JESSIE WILMORE MURTON
  Epitaph Written in Snow   161

STARR NELSON
  The Skeleton on the Shore   161

LOUISE TOWNSEND NICHOLL
  Refraction   162
  In Space the One Great Ornament   163
  Knowing What Time It Is at Night   163

GRACE FALLOW NORTON
  Phoenix   164

JOHN MYERS O'HARA
  Atropos   165

JAMES OPPENHEIM
  Tasting the Earth   166

SHAEMAS O'SHEEL
  Bagpipes   167

WINTHROP PALMER
  New York   167

JOSEPHINE PRESTON PEABODY
  Cradle Song   168

WILLIAM ALEXANDER PERCY
  Confidants   171

HAROLD TROWBRIDGE PULSIFER
  Of Little Faith   171

EDWIN QUARLES
  Threnody   172

ELIZABETH RANDALL-MILLS
  The Quick Still Center   173

BYRON HERBERT REECE
  Whose Eye Is on the Sparrow   174

LIZETTE WOODWORTH REESE
  In Time of Grief   174

CALE YOUNG RICE
  Old Age   175

ROSA COATES RICHARDS
  Weaver   176

MARGARET R. RICHTER
  Elegy for a Lost Continent   176

JESSIE B. RITTENHOUSE
  The Hawthorn   178

CLYDE ROBERTSON
  The Yellow Witch of Caribou   179

EDWIN ARLINGTON ROBINSON
  Flammonde   181

HENRY MORTON ROBINSON
  Week-End Love   184
  Second Wisdom   184

JAMES RORTY
  The Bell-Ringers   185
  End of Farce   185

COLEMAN ROSENBERGER
  A Memorial for Mr. Jefferson   187

DAVID ROSS
  Broadcast to the Scholars in the Eyrie   188

SYDNEY KING RUSSELL
  Invocation   189

I. L. SALOMON
  Fit Remembrance   189

HARRIET SAMPSON
  Freedom Considered   190

GEORGE SANTAYANA
  Ode to Mediterranean   191
  O World   192

LEW SARETT
  To a Wild Goose over Decoys   193
  Cattle Bells   194
  Four Little Foxes   194

JOHN SCHAFFNER
  An Island   195

CLINTON SCOLLARD
  As I Came Down from Lebanon   196

ANDERSON M. SCRUGGS
  Man Is Forever Lonely   197

FRANK DEMPSTER SHERMAN
  Bacchus   198

RUTH FORBES SHERRY
  Coronal: A Legend of the Annunciation   199

CONSTANCE LINDSAY SKINNER
  Indian Spring   200

ELEANOR SANDS SMITH
  Death Stirs the Arras   201

LEONORA SPEYER
  These Poems I Have So Loved   202
  Note to 'Fiddler's Farewell'   203
  The Weeper   203

LAWRENCE PERRY SPINGARN
  Rococo Summer   204

FLORENCE DICKINSON STEARNS
  Bargain   205

GEORGE STERLING
  Paris   205

HELEN FRITH STICKNEY
  From an Ivory Tower   206

A. M. SULLIVAN
  The Chronometer   207
  Counsel for Youth   208

ELDA TANASSO
  Morning without Malice   208

ANNE SOUTHERNE TARDY
  Sun through Window Shutters   209

MARY ATWATER TAYLOR
  The Little Progress   210

SARA TEASDALE
  Arcturus in Autumn   210

ROSEMARY THOMAS
  New Hampshire   211

DOROTHY BROWN THOMPSON
  In Time of Snow   211

EUNICE TIETJENS
  The Most-Sacred Mountain   212

RIDGELY TORRENCE
  Harvest Home   213
  Prothalamium   214
  Three O'Clock   214

CHARLES HANSON TOWNE
  Of One Self-Slain   215

VIRGINIA LYNE TUNSTALL
  April's Daughter   216

JEAN STARR UNTERMEYER
  Unshared Elegy   216

HAROLD VINAL
  Notation from Elba   218

ELEANOR GLENN WALLIS
  Summer Barely Heard   219

MAY WILLIAMS WARD
  My Little Sister   220

JAMES E. WARREN, JR.
  The Swan   220
  Bather Sleeping   221

TESSA SWEAZY WEBB
  Storm   222

WINIFRED WELLES
  The Two Twilights   222

JOHN HALL WHEELOCK
  Unison   223

MARGARET WIDDEMER
  High House   225

MARGUERITE WILKINSON
  Never Hurt the Proud   226

B. Y. WILLIAMS
  Of Foxes   227

GEORGE EDWARD WOODBERRY
  Wild Eden   228

CATHARINE MORRIS WRIGHT
  Travelers in the Orient   230

FREDERICK A. WRIGHT
  Letter to the City Clerk   231

HELEN M. WRIGHT
  Snow on Avenue B   232

MARGARET FREDERICKA WRIGHT
  Willow Tree   232

Contents

MARY J. J. WRINN
  Grecian Lamp Unearthed near Sparta   233

ELINOR WYLIE
  Hymn to Earth   234

FAY M. YAUGER
  Planter's Charm   236
  I Remember   238

MARGUERITE YOUNG
  The Funeral   239
  Voyager Man   239
  The Raven   240

Acknowledgments   243

Biographical Notes   249

Index of Poems   281

Index of First Lines   287

POETRY SOCIETY OF AMERICA
ANTHOLOGY

Marguerite Janvrin Adams

PRAYER IN AN ARCTIC SEASON

Having known other seasons, other faces,
faces illumined by the touch of peace,
from this stark winter and its arctic spaces
we ask release.

Against the gun's sharp speech, against the frost,
the hillock turned for crops that will not grow,
even against the eventual holocaust
that we must know,

give us cool reason to employ our hands
towards farther vision, and our hearts to this
new growth. Temper the sorrow of all lands
under such emphasis.

Sara Van Alstyne Allen

THE ZOO IN THE CITY

Enclose the lacquered, coiling snake
Within a web of glass.
Offer for his devious need
A subsidy of grass.

Hollow out the bitter stone.
Provide the bowl for a neat sea.
The sleek and polished city seal
Detects in this no irony.

Crowd into a music-box
A hundred birds to sing.
And measure out the humming air
For every slanting wing.

Circumscribe the panther's grace
Within a cell of steel and wire.
Dim to a dull processional
The stealthy pace, the hunter's fire.

Here between stone and rearing stone
Man adds a fillip to his feast,
Keeping to round his holiday
The netted bird, the futile beast.

Dorothy Alyea

PORTRAIT OF TWO UNHAPPY YOUNG PEOPLE

This passionate child, so much in love with folly,
With momentary joy, with kitten's play,
Giving a kiss with mistletoe and holly,
Another bauble for the holiday;
How should she know, who has no wish for proving
The strict division in a lover's mind—
An 'easy conquest' meaning lighter loving,
And 'chastity' a truer womankind.
With no such thoughtfulness will she give over,
But as a child goes coasting down a steep,
The bright snow flashing as the runners cover
The frozen ground, so swiftly will she heap
In the loose hands of some reluctant lover
The virtue he had rather she would keep.

John Williams Andrews

NEW WONDER

To me, between the all-absorbing wonders
Of birth and death, is come this woman-thing,
No substance born of comet-fires or thunders,
Light or the preparate earth, yet rendering
Changes unfancied in this pattern of days,
A new absorption, focussing the spirit
In concentration past all reasoning ways,
Past hope or fear, desire, reward or merit.

So if, in these rich hours; if, in this house,
Shaped by our common will; if, in these nights,
So full of moonlight along apple-boughs
 (Catching, just now, the late sun from the heights);
If, in this loneliness, where night and day,
Scarcely another voice than ours is heard:
Only the wind's voice; only, far away,
The crystal crying of a woodland bird;

If, in this singleness of life, I seem
Over-absorbed, believe, no casual thing
Preoccupies; rather, the imperious dream
Which life imposes where the narrow ring
Of sight and sound and anxious circumstance
Is drawn away. New wonder, creeping close,
Ordains attention, and immediate wants
Slough off and fade. Where the soul's silence grows,

Sense manufactures strangeness from a vein
Deeper than earth, deeper than wind or rain.

Mary Austin

THE EAGLE'S SONG

Said the Eagle:
When my time came
I was astonished
To find that there was death;
I felt cold sinking within me.

Alas, my home—
Shall I leave it?
All-beholding mountains,
From your snowy stations
Shall I see my house no more?

North I went,
Leaning on the wind:
Through the forest resounded
The cry of the wounded doe.

East I went,
Seeking
Where the white-hot dawn
Treads on the trail of morning blueness:
The wind brought me
The smell of death in my nostrils.

South I went,
Looking
For the place where there is no death:
I heard singing,
The sound of wailing for the dead.

West I went,
On the world-encompassing water:
Death's trail was before me.

People, O people,
It must be that we shall leave this pleasant earth.
Therefore let us make songs together,
Let us make a twine of songs.
With them we shall bind the Spirit
Fast to the middle heaven—
There at least it shall roam no more.
The white way of souls—
There at least it shall roam no more.
The white way of souls,
There shall be our home.

Karle Wilson Baker

I SHALL BE LOVED AS QUIET THINGS

I shall be loved as quiet things
Are loved—white pigeons in the sun,
Curled yellow leaves that whisper down
One after one;

The silver reticence of smoke
That tells no secret of its birth
Among the fiery agonies
That turn the earth;

Cloud-islands; reaching arms of trees;
The frayed and eager little moon
That strays unheeded through a high
Blue afternoon.

The thunder of my heart must go
Under the muffling of the dust—
As my grey dress has guarded it
The grasses must;

For it has hammered loud enough,
Clamored enough, when all is said:
Only its quiet part shall live
When I am dead.

Elsa Barker

THE TWO SELVES

Two selves have I that work not for the weal
Of one another, though they must abide
In the same house of life. One is the tried
Indomitable spirit made of steel,
Tempered by fire and cold from head to heel.
The other is the woman who is made
Of softest rose leaves, wistful and afraid,
Whose only armor is love's pure appeal.

Water and oil will blend before these two.
What hidden purpose of the Infinite
Has to these alien dwellers thus decreed
One narrow house of life the long years through?
The rose leaves rust the steel and weaken it,
The steel has torn the rose leaves till they bleed.

WHEN I AM DEAD

When I am dead and sister to the dust;
When no more avidly I drink the wine
Of human love; when the pale Proserpine
Has covered me with poppies, and cold rust
Has cut my lyre-strings, and the sun has thrust
Me underground to nourish the world-vine,
Men shall discover these old songs of mine,
And say: This woman lived—as poets must.

This woman lived and wore life as a sword
To conquer wisdom; this dead woman read
In the sealed Book of Love and underscored
The meanings. Then the sails of faith she spread,
And faring out for regions unexplored,
Went singing down the River of the Dead.

Isabel Harriss Barr

ANSWER FROM ASSISI

Can you divide seed,
Or apportion marrow,
To sum up the need
Of eagle and sparrow?

Will deeds that you sow
For good or for evil
Be grist for the crow
Or blossom for weavel?

Must hate first be ended
To bring forth good fruit
And the earth be so tended
Compassion will root?

And if in the growing
The heart has returned
The Giver's bestowing—
Is the harvest earned?

From humility
Such flowering came.
One in Assisi
Knew Love was its name.

Laura Benét

CROWNING

Crown us who make within,
Our thrones and places high,
Though the gold crown be thin,
Let it be light as sky.

And may the aureole shine,
The rounded circlet glow,
That we be kings in fine
Before our overthrow.

One crown, one life, one hour—
Decree in justice, Lord,
That none usurp the power
Of our so brief award!

Stephen Vincent Benét

AMERICAN NAMES

I have fallen in love with American names,
The sharp gaunt names that never get fat,
The snakeskin-titles of mining-claims,
The plumed war-bonnet of Medicine Hat,
Tucson and Deadwood and Lost Mule Flat.

Seine and Piave are silver spoons,
But the spoonbowl-metal is thin and worn,
There are English counties like hunting-tunes
Played on the keys of a postboy's horn,
But I will remember where I was born.

I will remember Carquinez Straits,
Little French Lick and Lundy's Lane,
The Yankee ships and the Yankee dates
And the bullet-towns of Calamity Jane.
I will remember Skunktown Plain.

I will fall in love with a Salem tree
And a rawhide quirt from Santa Cruz,
I will get me a bottle of Boston sea
And a blue-gum nigger to sing me blues.
I am tired of loving a foreign muse.

Rue des Martyrs and Bleeding-Heart-Yard,
Senlis, Pisa and Blindman's Oast,
It is a magic ghost you guard;
But I am sick for a newer ghost—
Harrisburg, Spartanburg, Painted Post.

Henry and John were never so,
And Henry and John were always right?
Granted, but when it was time to go
And the tea and the laurels had stood all night,
Did they never watch for Nantucket Light?

I shall not rest quiet in Montparnasse.
I shall not lie easy in Winchelsea.
You may bury my body in Sussex grass,
You may bury my tongue at Champmédy.
I shall not be there. I shall rise and pass.
Bury my heart at Wounded Knee.

William Rose Benét

TWO NORTH SHORE POEMS

Trammeled Swimmer

Sleek from silk water the angled arm. The sun
Shook crinkling sequins. Slipping ripples burned.
With thew and heart and blood and thought as one
         His body turned.

He twisted on his back, and at the noon
Thrashed sun-browned feet; then lay, and let the bound
Of blue absorb him, like the faint day-moon
         A perfect round.

Floating infinity, for now the blue
Was cloudless, he was lifted to a height
No rock, no shore, no sea-horizon knew.
         He lived in light.

A Knowing profound; from all life's friction free;
Higher than flyer; aloft, alone, elate;
One with all infinite possibility;
         Disjoined from fate,

And reaching almost . . . seeming about to reach . . .
He twisted prone; arm flashed and body sped.
"What were you swimming?" his friend asked, at the beach.
         "The crawl," he said.

Late Summer

When the aster's smoke-blue
And the mountain-ash is gold,
Many old things are new,
Many new things are old.
There's a frost with the dew
And the first hint of cold.

There's Cassandra the crow
In a coign of the bay;
And the sun appears to know
What the surf seems to say:
That the lovers too must go
With the high wings away.

Lift your face to the sun,
Gray your eyes out to sea.
Past and present as one
In this pause seem to be,
With the new-born, long-done,
And the bonds on the free.

So the grief laid on you
Like a legend seems told
Where the old faith is new
And all new pangs are old,
When the aster's smoke-blue
And the mountain-ash is gold.

Gertrude Ryder Bennett

TROPICAL FISH

A tank through which you glide and gleam
Is all you know of lake or stream.
How limited your world! Your sky
Might be a person passing by.
You dart across a bed of sand
Arranged and measured out by hand.
Your vegetation, water-grass
Within horizons made of glass.

Yet here is mating, here is birth
As actual as on our earth.
Ecstatic motion, hunger, fear,
The elemental things are here.
For space is boundless after all,
And never is a place too small
To entertain, where there is breath,
The vast experience of death.

John Peale Bishop

ENCOUNTER

In the rags of a wind
A man who was proud
Called out to me, Wait!
The low light was late
When he came: I have sinned
And must say it aloud!

Together we walked;
The late light was yellow
On the inland marsh,
Cold yellow and harsh
Where cattails stalked
And salt grass was sallow.

I heard his heart beat
Upon each word.
What he said was this:
I have given a kiss
As Iscariot's sweet
When he hurt our Lord.

He was done and a silence
Came down on my stare.
His eyes were dark O's
And a great bird rose
Through the tarnished air
Of those sluggish islands.

He lifted a face
Which crowned thorns had bled.
But I said nothing
Of my great loathing
And for my embrace
He held his head.

He had no shame:
I heard the blood drip
Through the white rib bone
Of his skeleton.
And I stood with cold lip
Whose sin was the same.

John Black

SONG COMES LIKE A FRUSTRATED FLOWER

Song comes like a frustrated flower,
Tortuous, twining among rocks,
Rebel, fortuitous to shocks,
And growing, hour by hour.

Nor any right way yet to grow,
Nor any wrong way love to lift,
Only with passion now to drift,
Only with spring to blow.

Song comes in all my love's despite,
Oh, love so great; oh, song so small!
Song comes, a miracle of light,
And glitters over all.

Elizabeth Bohm

TRACKS

Two azure lines traverse the town.
They grow to two lines out of one
And far away upon the plain
They grow back into one again.

The people give them little heed.
From time to time a storm of speed
Rises and roars along the ground
And engines, carried in its sound,
Flash long necklaces of cars . . .
No more than shooting summer stars
Do they affect the stores and streets,
The yards alive with flapping sheets,
The men, the dust. It all goes on
As usual when the train is gone.

And yet beyond the farthest shacks
Proceed those bright mysterious tracks,
Growing out of one to two
And back to one line, sharp and blue,
Pointing with an arrowy light
To something out of sight.

Amy Bonner

HOUSE LONG KNOWN

This place is familiar—
    by the sea,
With wide lawns and upper
    balconies,
And darkness under the
    eaves;
And the agony of trying
    to press
Through narrow doors and
    low apertures,
Along underground tunnels
    and platforms,
Ways fraught with discomfort
    and despair;
  Finally, an exit
    is found
Where the imprisoned one
    again is free
To follow the mind's
    freedom,
To walk, to float
    along the lawns,
    up and down slopes, hills,
The body forgotten,
    the hazards shed—
The house long known, found,
    the terrain familiar,
    the people, the sea.

Carl John Bostelmann

HARPER'S FERRY

Something immortal is sequestered here
In this cleft between hills, in the taut air:
A midnight mutiny, a morning fear,
The heavy footfall on a scaffold stair,
The tread of military feet. Here peace
Is broken by the sharp insurgent sound
Of a bugle blowing. Quick sounds increase
As tumultuous thunders shake the ground.

A peculiar terror inhabits this
Rural asylum, where fate touched the drum
That called a nation to its precipice
And brought a madman back from martyrdom,

A terror of the blood, a memory
Of strange historic incidents come down
To a meek people—of a wrath that we
Remember as a certain fool named Brown.

Bianca Bradbury

FARMER'S WIFE

Taking him, I understand
That I am marrying the land,
An old beloved liaison,
She mistress, I the wife of one
Born of her love and bred of her bone.

And I must learn, and learn this soon,
Who it is, who always yields
To the smiling tyranny of fields.
By his arms' loosening, I know
He turns from me to the window's glow
Where the earth is sleeping with the moon.
For in her moods and tantrums, live
The springtimes I can never give.
Plow and harrow, reap and sow,
The ritual of love possessed
His father's fathers, all their lives.
I, with those dim, complaisant wives
Content myself with second best.

Ann Bradshaw

ONE BLACK CROW

Blacker than black of the plum-tree bough
On which he sat, the lone crow looked
Beady-eyed at a small child staring
Back. She hoped this crow could talk.
Gray sky, frozen ground and silence.
Expecting the miracle, she stood quite still.
One flake of snow fell and then another.
Soon the ground looked like salt and pepper.
Then salt only. She never forgot
One black crow on a plum tree bough
And snow at its very beginning.

Anna Hempstead Branch

IN THE BEGINNING WAS THE WORD

It took me ten days
To read the Bible through.
Then I saw what I saw,
And I knew what I knew.

I would rise before the dawn,
When the stars were in the sky;
I would go and read the Book,
Till the sun rode high.

In the slience of the room
I would read with a will.
I was one who had climbed
To an high, burning hill.

At dusk I fell asleep
With my head on the page.
Then I woke—then I read—
Till an hour seemed an age.

For a great wind blows
Through Ezekiel and John,
They are all one flesh
That the Spirit breathes upon.

And suddenly the words
Seemed to quicken and to shine;
They glowed like the bread,
They purpled like the wine.

Like bread that had been wheat
In a thousand ample plains,
Sown and harvested by men
From the suns—from the rains.

Like wine that had been grapes
In a thousand vineyards strong—
That was trampled by men's feet
With a shout, with a song.

Like the Bread, like the Wine,
That we eat with one accord—
The body and the blood
Of the supper of the Lord.

And the wine may be old
And the wine may be new—
But it all is the Lord's—
And I knew what I knew.

For a great wind blows
Through Ezekiel and John,
They are all one flesh
That the Spirit breathes upon.

And a letter is a power,
And a name is a rune—
And an alphabet, my friends,
Is a strange and ancient tune.

And each letter is a throne
From which fearful splendors stream—
I could see them flash like fire
With an arch-angelic gleam.

And within each word a city
Shone more far than eye could reach—
Where the people glowed like stars
With a great new speech.

And each city was an angel,
And they sang with one accord—
Crying, "Holy, holy, holy,"
In the presence of the Lord.

The Book felt like flesh,
It would breathe—it would sing—
It would throb beneath my hand
Like a bird, like a wing.

It would cry, it would groan,
It would shout and complain,—
It would seem to climb a hill
With its solemn stress of pain.

It would grapple with fierce powers,
With a deep interior strife.
It would seem to heave and lift
With a terrible, glad life.

And my flesh was in the Book,
And its blood was in me;
I could feel it throb within,
As plain as it could be.

I was filled with its powers,
And I cried all alone,
"The Lord is in the tomb,
And my body is the stone."

I was anguished, I was dumb,
When the powers began to move,
That shall stir the aching ground,
That shall shake the earth with love.

Then my flesh, which was the stone,
Felt the hills begin to lift.
The seas shook and heaved,
And the stars began to shift.

And the words rushed on
And each letter was a throne.
They swept through my flesh,
Through my brain, through my bone.

With a great, fearful rush
I felt it clean through.
Oh, I saw what I saw,
And I knew what I knew.

And I swung one side
When the ghostly power began.
Then the Book stood up—
And I saw it was a Man.

For a great wind blows
Through Ezekiel and John.
They are all one flesh
That the Spirit breathes upon.

It took me ten days
To read the Bible through—
Then I saw what I saw,
And I knew what I knew.

Florence Kerr Brownell

STRAWBERRY MARK

Was it because it was a long summer, the season lived under
    the tree
From cocoon of bud to frayed blossom
With afterward the fruit slow in shaping,
Later, ripe-fallen on the ground?

With the child-beat under my heart,
Was it because—watching the leaf in cycle of celadon to rust—
The eyes were sky-held
Where birds flew?

The pears are yellowed now, thudding under the tree;
    this has been a swift season.
So soon the alarm—squadron took flight:
In bird formation, I am told.
Each trip, a few never return.

He took up flying before the winter of matriculation . . .
Was it because it was a long summer,
My eyes sky-held?

Nancy Bruff

THE ONE AMBASSADOR

A prayer is a measureless thing.
It is the unknown x of mathematicians
The lost dimension of the savant
And that most elusive perfect note
For which musicians strive.
It is the word that poets search.

A prayer is a weightless message bearing
The lone stamp of identity
Unique and solitary.
Freely given, or wrenched from us
In extremity—a prayer is an envoy
Too quickened to be lost.

Elizabeth J. Buchtenkirk

BLACK SOLDIER

Up from a darkness, darker yet,
And tethered still to his despair,
The black man in his anxious sweat
Moves against the weighted air.

Heavy with his sorrow-song,
Slow-footed, braced against the tide,
His skin the total of his wrong,
Knowing the adder-sting of pride,

He, rising up from where he slept,
Takes in his flesh the tolerant steel,
Here where no racial tears are wept,
Here where the wounded soul may heal.

Helen Burlin

CATERPILLAR

The grass has come alive.
One blade converts to worm
Green streaked with yellow streak.
A manifestation in minor form
Shunts and nuzzles from peak to peak.

Sightless he swings
A helpless head
A head in air
Seeking his next abode,
Then shoves his linear structure there.

Pauses, so returns again.
Back and forth, forth and back
I watch the futile trek
And think, with all of world to take,
Men, how many, whirl on a penny.

Struthers Burt

WE ARE WONDERFUL, WE ARE WISE

We are wonderful, we are wise,
Masters of space and speed and echoing spheres;
We have killed our young men marvelously for years.

Lords of the earth, of metal, and of ease,
We have made a thin blue coffin of the skies,
And of the high fine business of the seas
A wet and narrow burial;
We are wonderful,
We are wise!

Beat drums, for we have even conquered death
And made him young;
Death is no longer old, but a young man flying.
Beat drums, your sound may hush the crying
Of the old earth for the young men dying.

Youth has no time to watch the wheeling star,
Or roundness of the moon, so made for death.
The dawn is terror where the young men are,
And golden hills where once the harpist stood,
Are gold no longer for the harpist's blood.
Beat drums for the end of young desire.

We are wonderful, we are wise,
But we have made an end to youthful singing.
Will any young man, watchful, chide the light,
That is too long contented with the night,
When he would rise to visions and delight?
What will he wake to but the sound of metal ringing?

We are wonderful, we are wise,
We have given wings and engines to our tears;
We have killed our young men marvelously for years.

Richard Burton

BLACK SHEEP

From their folded mates they wander far,
Their ways seem harsh and wild;
They follow the beck of a baleful star,
Their paths are dream-beguiled.

Yet haply they sought but a wider range,
Some loftier mountain-slope,
And little recked of the country strange
Beyond the gates of hope.

And haply a bell with a luring call
Summoned their feet to tread
Midst the cruel rocks, where the deep pitfall
And the lurking snare are spread.

Maybe, in spite of their tameless days
Of outcast liberty,
They're sick at heart for the homely ways
Where their gathered brothers be.

And oft at night, when the plains fall dark
And the hills loom large and dim,
For the Shepherd's voice they mutely hark,
And their souls go out to him.

Meanwhile, "Black sheep! Black sheep!" we cry,
Safe in the inner fold;
And maybe they hear, and wonder why,
And marvel, out in the cold.

Frances Westgate Butterfield

LE PRINTEMPS EMPOISSONNE

France must have dogwood, too,
And Belgium apple trees
And doubtless it is true
That bombs strike such as these.

But what a hideous waste
To blast an oriole,
When less indecent haste
Might blast a human soul.

War breeds such bitter fruit
That spring, so fair this year,
Is poisoned at the root
With paralyzing fear

That drives me to my knees
With thoughts, as through a trance,
Of Belgian dogwood trees
Of apple blooms in France.

Witter Bynner

DEFEAT

On a train in Texas German prisoners eat
With white American soldiers, seat by seat,
While black American soldiers sit apart,
The white man eating meat, the black men heart.
Now, with that other war a century done,
Not the live north but the dead south has won,
Not yet a riven nation comes awake.
Whom are we fighting this time, for God's sake?
Mark well the token of the separate seat:
It is again ourselves whom we defeat.

Melville Cane

BEHIND DARK SPACES

Somewhere, behind dark spaces,
Light races.
Pressure
Of rushing light
Tears a fissure
Across night,
A crack
In black less black.

Gradual starry withdrawal,
Cool of sky's vague pool,
Faint disclosure of rose,
Blue palely filtering through,

Under grim black, dim
Earth-green,—
Emerging scene.

Out of shreds, out of seeds, of utter grey,
Ultimate, brightly-woven, high-flowering day.

ASKEW, WE ASK YOU

Gertrude—there's a good old scout!
What's it what's it all about?
Hear a tortured hemisphere
Begging you to make it clear.
Drop a clue or slip a hint
Touching on the what-you-print,
What-you-print and what-there's-in't.

Abdicate the role of sibyl,
At your secret let us nibble.
Pray divulge, reveal, disclose
In communicable prose
Why a rose a rose a rose.

Are you wilfully obscure?
Are you puerile or mature?
We are anything but sure.

Are you spoofing or profound?
Is there sense within the sound?
Will you properly expound?

Is your highly Orphic text
Meant for this world or the next?
We concede we are perplexed.

Is it genius, is it sham?
Will you answer kindly, Ma'am?

Are you hollow or a mine?
One remembes Shakespeare's line:
"Sermons lie concealed in Stein."

Gertrude answers, slightly bored:
"Gertrude is her own reward."

HYMN TO NIGHT

Now it grows dark.
Red goes
Out of the rose;
Out of the lawn
Green's withdrawn;
Each buttercup now yields
Its gold from blurring fields;
Larkspur and sky surrender
Blue wonder.

We were dark within, we relied
For our strength on the nourishing sun;
Now it is under and gone.
Now, as the light grows duller,
We, who had flourished on color,
Stand, in the ever-deepening shade,
Bereft, dismayed.

We were dark within, it was death
We saw, we had never seen
Within the dark, we had never known
The spark, the vital breath.
If only we had known
That black is neither loss nor lack
But holds the essential seed
Of mortal hope and need!

Now sheltering dusk,
Shepherd of color and light for dawns unending,
Tends the holy task.

Praise be to black, the benign,
No longer malign,
Prolonger of days!

Praise the preserver of shine,
The keeper of blaze!

Praise Night,
Forever praise
Savior Night,
Who surely stays
The arm of time,
Who guards the flame,
Who hoards the light.

Praised be the Night.

Sara King Carleton

CATHEDRAL

No drawing of the planner's art
Of carving stone or setting beam
Reveals the purpose of the heart,
The architecture of a dream.

No text can tell how Beauty grows
Beyond the craftsman's careful tool,
How windows blossoming into rose
Escape the hand, exceed the rule.

Translated into Time and Space
These vaulted aisles and cloisters wear
An actual Pentecostal grace,
Granite evolving into prayer.

Bliss Carman

A VAGABOND SONG

There is something in the autumn that is native to my blood—
Touch of manner, hint of mood;
And my heart is like a rhyme,
With the yellow and the purple and the crimson keeping time.

The scarlet of the maples can shake me like a cry
Of bugles going by.
And my lonely spirit thrills
To see the frosty asters like a smoke upon the hills.

There is something in October sets the gypsy blood astir;
We must rise and follow her,
When from every hill of flame
She calls and calls each vagabond by name.

Madison Cawein

DESERTED

The old house leans upon a tree
Like some old man upon a staff:
The night wind in its ancient porch
Sounds like a hollow laugh.

The heaven is wrapped in flying clouds
As grandeur cloaks itself in gray:
The starlight flitting in and out,
Glints like a lanthorn ray.

The dark is full of whispers. Now
A fox-hound howls: and through the night,
Like some old ghost from out its grave,
The moon comes misty white.

Katherine Garrison Chapin

LOVE BELEAGUERED

This is the last refuge I can give you
Yet you will find no peace, not even here.
Nor in the solace of my arms that hold you,
You will find no safety anywhere.

Perhaps for moments, perhaps forgetting
The clamor of anger that rages across the sky
You will believe that here, in tenderness begetting
Comfort for your heartache is peace. That is a lie.

Love is not a drug for endless sleeping.
It is not quiet for one raidless night.
Love is a fever and a stir, a leaping
Siren in the blood, a torturing delight.

And if you come to me, come with this knowing,
O my dear, the unrest is mine. It is upon me; I wait
With all the whistles of destruction blowing,
To share this last joy, sweet and desperate.

Thomas Caldecot Chubb

WILD DUCK SONG

Once upon a time—once in Georgia—
I saw a great horde
Of wild duck flying
Like the lightning of the Lord;

I saw wild duck flying;
I heard their wings beat
With a noise like the pistons
Of an engine running sweet,

With a sound like brooding thunder,
With a swift, sure thrum,
With a throb like singing pulse beats,
Or a strong, rolled drum.

I saw them flying
Without swerve to left or right.
Their necks were stretched straight,
And their bellies flashed white;

A hundred, a thousand
In a great dark swarm
Till the sky was streaked and smoky
As before a storm.

I remember the place:
A wide, shallow lake
Gleamed in the sunlight
Like the cast skin of a snake.

There were lily pads as brown
As an old felt hat,
And tangled sedgy grasses.
The shores were low and flat.

More and more they came,
And their wings beat a tune
As wild as any saga,
As weird as any rune,

Scrawling ancient magic,
And then they had swept on.
The empty sky gulped them.
They were utterly gone.

And there followed such a stillness,
You could hear your heart stop,
Or a dry grass blade bend,
Or a single leaf drop.

Gertrude Claytor

INDIAN WIFE

On Sunday when the stern bells called for prayer,
Kneeling in silence they would find her there.
All through the sermon, folded in her lap,
Her strong calm hands lay still;
And yet her mind, a vagrant bird,
Flew out, escaped her will.
One who was old and wise,
Watching her eyes,
Had heard sharp wind, felt cold reach to his marrow,
And seen again, as in his frightened youth, a flying arrow.

Beneath a tallow dip, she stitched a seam,
With every thread a chain to bind her there,
A prisoner by the open cabin door,
A prisoner in the stiff cane-bottom chair.

How soft are doe-skin shoes,
As light as leaves;
Her leather boots were harsh and cramped her feet;
How sweet the smell of fire on the wind,
And soft the touch of doe-skin for a gown.
There was no peace for her between straight walls,
No rest within the little bustling town.
Her hands were beautiful as bending boughs,
And brown as early autumn leaves are brown.

One night when the moon was curved and slender
And frost had whitened on the dying grass,
She went away as softly as a whisper,
Passing the threshold as a shade might pass.
Now open on its rusting hinges
The unbound door swings back, then to and fro,
Calling the rain to fall aross the doorsill,
Calling to all free things to come and go.

Catherine Cate Coblentz

HAKLUYT AND THE "ENGLISH VOYAGES"

Salt of the sea was ever on his lips;—
Creaking of English sails and cold spume lifting
Across his cheek from wraiths of outbound ships
That filled the night with their eternal drifting . . .
Westward and ever west to wind-swept lands,
And sweet horizons, on and ever on,
These ghostly fleets that paused on misted strands
Anchored in darkness, fading with the dawn.

This dreamer held in port, in four walls placed,
His sails, the edges of the curtain blowing,

His far-off visions, simple words well traced
From bronzed pilots to his fireside going.
And yet the sea was there . . . from Hakluyt's pen
It surges still—it sings of Englishmen.

Stanton A. Coblentz

THE WOODS SHALL NOT BE LONELY

The woods shall not be lonely
   When man has slipped away,
Leaving no token, only
   Dark timbers that decay.

They shall not miss his bustling,
   His noisy stir, his cries.
No autumn sea-wind, rustling,
   Shall weep at his demise.

But in the cool, dim hollows
   The ancient peace shall fall.
Squirrels shall hop, and swallows
   Go winging over all.

And fern and moss and quiet,
   Shadows and sun shall blend,
In groves where bluejays riot
   And antlered bodies bend.

With houseless tenants only
   To flit and soar and play,
The woods shall not be lonely
   When man has slipped away.

Robert P. Tristram Coffin

THE SECRET HEART

Across the years he could recall
His father one way best of all.

In the stillest hour of night
The boy awakened to a light.

Half in dreams, he saw his sire
With his great hands full of fire.

The man had struck a match to see
If his son slept peacefully.

He held his palms each side the spark
His love had kindled in the dark.

His two hands were curved apart
In the semblance of a heart.

He wore, it seemed to his small son,
A bare heart on his hidden one,

A heart that gave out such a glow
No son awake could bear to know.

It showed a look upon a face
Too tender for the day to trace.

One instant, it lit all about,
And then the secret heart went out.

But it shone long enough for one
To know that hands held up the sun.

Gladys Cromwell

THE CROWNING GIFT

I have had courage to accuse;
And a fine wit that could upbraid;
And a nice cunning that could bruise;
And a shrewd wisdom, unafraid
Of what weak mortals fear to lose.

I have had virtue to despise
The sophistry of pious fools;
I have had firmness to chastise;
And intellect to make me rules,
To estimate and exorcise.

I have had knowledge to be true;
My faith could obstacles remove.
But now, by failure taught anew,
I would have courage now to love,
And lay aside the strength I knew.

Henry Dalton

SHORT STORY

For it was winter now,
And what they had not spoken
When pear blossoms snowflaked downward
Would be easier—or so they thought.

Light of December afternoons
Lay like a revelation on familiar objects:

Woodcut, teakwood box, the chipped grey street.
They stood at the window, faces rapt,
Watching the snow pear blossom downward.

Clear days came and still they waited,
Shaping the casual phrase to steady line,
Although the pear blossom month,
The things that absence held,
And all that winter clarifies
Had trembled out upon omniscient fingers.

Wisdom it may have been, or fear:
They did not speak.
Without a word they strode past naked pear trees
Into the formal dusk,
Noting how the tall weeds reach for stars.

Earl Daniels

SMALL APOCALYPSE

The sound heard
is not the sound that matters:

neither clocks ticking
invisible in darkness,
nor, in solemn midnight,
tower bells striking;

these are of small moment,
if one waking ear listen.

Think rather upon clocks
where the doors have been shut
ticking, the sounds lost
because no one heard them;

this, in the long run,
is matter for meditation.

Gustav Davidson

THE GOLDEN LEOPARD

In terror of its own delight
The golden leopard of desire
With urge and pace that never tire
Tramples the earth with feet of fire
And through the ambush of the night
Faces the dawn with eyes afright.

The jungle heavy on its back
The seas' grey vastness thunder-loud
Spreading before it like a shroud
The golden leopard trapped and cowed
Fearing it knows not what attack
Stands dazed and baffled in its track.

MORTAL HUNGER

Now more than ever, more than ever now
I look on death with unaffrighted eyes.
The bloom, the blossom and the fruited bough
Quickening in the sun of cloudless skies
Will not outlast the summer. This I know.
And all that wakes and dreams, struggles and dies—
Shapes, odors, passions; storm and fog and snow—
How good that these should pass! How good and wise!
For life that, with the intake of each breath,
Moves to no end, knows neither joy nor grief.

The rare, the bright, the perilous is brief.
Beauty itself is but the pearl of death.
And though we yearn for some eternal sign,
That only which is mortal is divine.

Mary Carolyn Davies

HUNGER

In that strange city
    Of being poor,
I have lived all my life
    And more:

I have lived out from myself
    And from this place,
Out through time,
    Through space.

I know what others suffered
    Before me:
No one who is hungry
    Can be quite free.

That is the only suffering there is,
    Or was before,
Or will be, ever—
    Only being poor.

To lose a lover does not
    Shake the soul
Like a wet and broken shoe,
    Or an empty bowl,

Like the fear of no roof at night,
    And no hand to aid,
And most of all the fear
    Of being afraid.

Afraid of man because
    I have not that shield,
And the sword, of a small, round coin
    To wield.

Soul agony is sad,
    But this is worse:
To be broken by the number
    Of pennies in a purse.

ON BECOMING A BOOK

Time, I am small and easy to defeat,
    Some day I'll be a book upon a shelf
    In someone's room. And there'll be no myself:
No brown bobbed hair, no blue, wide eyes, no feet
To dance, dance! and no rebel heart to beat
    And thunder drowning all the thundering
    The arrogant city to my door can bring,
No mouth remembering all life's hidden sweet.

I, who have been so loved, will be a book!
    How merciless—and oh, how strange it seems!
Open the book, then, breathing one, and look
    With loving eyes at my small, hoarded dreams.
I who must, greedy, hear "I love you" said
Beg you to like my songs, when I am dead.

Julia Johnson Davis

JOHN

W'en de Lawd chose his 'ciples, Peter wuz de fus',
    Den he pick up Andrew too.
Jeems an' John wuz a-settin' close by,
    An' he says to 'em, "I needs you."
Philip an' Tholomew he done call,
    An' de Jeems dat wuz Alph'us' son,
Oh dey wuz de goodes' men dere wuz—
    But John wuz de likeliest one.

    Oh de Lawd love John de bes' of all,
    John wuz de likeliest one.

Peter wuz heavybuilt, Andrew wuz spar',
    An' Jeems wuz inbetween,
Matthew wuz de one that carried mos' weight,
    Philip wuz good and lean.
Oh Thomas had er straight back, Jude he was tall,
    Dey wuz good ter look upon,
But John wuz jes' like a picter in a book,
    John wuz de likeliest one.

Oh de Lawd love John de bes' of all,
John wuz de likeliest one.

Peter wuz de rock fo ter buil' de church,
    Andrew wuz one of de beams,
Matthew an' Tholomew dey wuz j'ists,
    So wuz Philip an' Jeems.
Thomas an' Simon an' Jude wuz de walls,
    An' de seats fo' ter set upon,
But John wuz de winder whar de light come in,
    John wuz de likeliest one.

    Oh de Lawd love John de bes' of all,
    John wuz de likeliest one.

TO AN ASS

Sure-footed, tireless, born to servitude,
Before the horse was tamed you toiled for man,
Your patient strength has borne him down the rude
And devious ways of earth since time began.
And yet how scornfully he speaks your name,
Measuring his ignoble mind by you,
"An ass!"—the words are but a cry of shame,
Flung out to give some stupid dolt his due.

Be patient, humble beast, and take men's scorning,
It is their way, and you are not the first
To give them aid and succor in the morning,
And find yourself at night a thing accurst.
Remember still that when the way was barred,
You, only, saw the angel of the Lord.

Elmer Dean

THE STALLION

The polished and proud-necked one,
stamping and neighing,
startles the moon-eyed cow.
The man's mind slips from his plow
to love and girls Maying.

The red mare answers her lord
and he glitters with power.
His hoofs cut deep in the sod.
There is storm in the great sire's blood
and the colts bunch and cower.

Apple trees let down their bloom
on the king going under.
He has stain-of-the-sun on his thighs
and a star between his bold eyes—
and his own kind of thunder.

August Derleth

LOST CHILD

Lingers long as time,
forever:
here in night, the smoke-held park,
where yellow arc-lights glow,
dispel the dark,
tree-shadow broken at a moonlit wall,
lingers here the child, the lost child
and his childhood—
where screech owls call:

lonely as the sound of rain
on fallen leaves,
the water sound adrip from eaves
November nights:
hearing still retreating faint,
the voice of youth in shrill, in distant cry:
Run, my good sheep, run!
in sound of voice that says:
I'm ready now. I'm coming.
And nobody comes.

Spring nights, fall nights,
where Apil evening never ends,

where autumn falls, October never falls away:
    time lends
eternity; here stays the dream
inviolably—in smoky village air,
the streetlights' glow in leaves,
wind's lonely sound.
House, street, and wind-bent tree
compose a world to be
forever, a place of things to touch, to see:
fist-clenched and bitter-eyed,
where still the lone, lost child
plays, dreams, cradles his mind
half-fearful in the shadows,
and asks of the circumscribed, blind
world: *only be kind.*

WILD APPLES
Thoreau in the Midwest: May, 1861

Calamus budded in the bottomland,
the lilacs blooming, and the wild crabapple:
rivers swollen with water from the north,
snow water, and the whippoorwills,
as once before, sing in the dusk . . .

Eighty years since he crossed Wisconsin
into Minnesota, along wild rivers—
cold to the council of the Sioux
at Redwood, who had expected to be warmed:
cold to the flash and show,
cold even to the Little Crow
exchanging words with him.—Thoreau!
Thoreau dying.

The Mississippi indolent with late spring:
country of larks, redwings, hawks,
wild pigeons, where he hunted nests
and gophers, and at last—
lo! the wild crabapple!

> *"Half-fabulous to me . . .*
> *I began to notice from the cars a tree*
> *with handsome rose-colored flowers.*
> *Eight miles west of the Falls,*
> *I touched it, smelled it,*
> *secured a lingering corymb of the flowers,*
> *remarkable for their delicious odor . . ."*

Sweet on the air, crabapple,
wild crabapple cloud of pink on country lane,
on rind of hill:
> *"Indigenous,*
> *like the Indians . . ."*
> The May wind
in their branches, moonlight
white in the enlarging whiteness of the night
on the rose corymbs—
his footsteps passing,
spectral, hushed sound in muted air; touching,
smelling—lover of bird, wood, sky—
(with one year left in which to die).

Fifth Month again. Where now
I walk beneath the old new-leafing bough—
underfoot bergamotte, the violet,
picking morels where I go—
upon the air the wild perfume,
the pink crab's bloom,
the tree an alien visitation at the line-fence—
I think of him, Thoreau.

The wild, indigenous American tree,—
so it must have seemed to him,
the indigenous American,
the man forever young . . .

> *"Not an assured inhabitant of earth . . .*
> *not quite earthy . . . something tender*
> *and divine about him."*

Lilacs in the dooryards,
in the deep woods, spikenard;
in the bottoms budded
calamus, and water-lilies yellow on the sloughs;
at field's edge, the pasture line,
wood's rim, the tawny tree,
the cloud of pink against unclouded sky,
as eighty years gone by . . .

> *"Half-fabulous to me . . .*
> *I began to notice from the cars a tree*
> *with handsome rose-colored flowers . . ."*

—words clinging to the mind
like scent far-scattered by the heart
of Thoreau, Thoreau dying, his feet on earth
last, lingering, to trace the trackless
path into the enormous last unseen wonder,
hearing the bee's sound, the killdeer's crying,
hearing the heart of the continent beating
in the sweet land,
he walked, dying.

> *"Not an assured inhabitant of earth . . .*
> *not quite earthy . . . something tender*
> *and divine about him . . . Indigenous,*
> *like the Indians . . ."*

". . . a lingering corymb of the flowers:"

—so with scent the heart bemusing
another generation's hours.

Samuel A. DeWitt

QUATRAINS FOR A BANK CASHIER

Enough that you must turn your days to discs
    Of jaundiced metal, telling one by one,
For surer fortunes and for lesser risks,
    With all the tense devotion of a nun.

Enough to die with this, when knowing more:
    How flowers are golden with no weight of gold,
And how beyond horizons lies a store
    Of treasure that no treasury can hold . . .

George Dillon

ADDRESS TO THE DOOMED
(From "The Flowering Stone")

I.

Say it is life that matters. Say the bone
And flesh that blazoned it are but a book
Mislaid, forgotten, and the meaning known.
I will believe, but I have lived to look
On the cold body of the beautiful dead,
White and immobile, as the moon is air—
The imperious heart being strangely quieted,
And the proud spirit flown I know not where.
Say it is earth again. Let it be hid
In ruined leaves. Account it as the dust
That quarrels not with doom and never did,
And reckon me among the quick who must.

Yet would I sleep tonight at the rose's root,
Seeing what time has trampled underfoot.

III.

I see how the forgetful earth replies,
Though plundered yearly, to the year's warm humour,
And leads new life, to stand with innocent eyes,
Unwarmed, unweaned, upon the sill of summer.
I see her trust and her betrayal clearly—
The beaks of shivering birds put up to beg,
The hawthorn bloom upon the branch too early,
The snake unwinding from the stolen egg.
Yet since the heart's dismay were but a shadow
Weightless on earth as of a flying wing,
Or autumn leaf upon a flowering meadow
Caught in the quick machinery of Spring—
Let the doomed brave be born ad slapped to breath:
I take these tidings to my master Death.

IX.

The earth is honored, for she keeps your history—
Her paths are lovely, for they show your way;
Her tombs are fragrant, for they tell your mystery,
Ambiguous tenant of the simple clay.
Metal and adamant, the heavens wheeling
Above the wayward ball look down unmoved—
Yet here the rock is disarrayed, revealing
What Time has murdered and what men have loved.
As a lost hunter in the howling north
Who borrows refuge where a camp has been—
The bed of pine-boughs and the smoldering hearth—
So have you found one planet warm and green:
A home till spring, a hearth to build a fire on
Against that blizzard blowing stone and iron.

Allan D. Dowling

THE ARROW'S DEATH

The target smiles because
it knows by heavenly laws
it is the arrow's grave.

the arrow shrieks, and lo!
as it flies thru the air;
itself it cannot save.

The flashing circles grow;
the arrow shrieks, and, lo!
it enters deep, and dies.

It has fulfilled its aim;
it has avoided shame;
in rigid peace it lies.

Jane Dransfield

THE GREAT SQUARE

On this September night, alone within
this house built lonely on a hill, by light
of lamp I trace upon the charted page
which stems from Ptolemy and Ulugh Beg,
the four great stars that form the Autumn Square
     Alpheratz   *Menkib*
     Algenib   *Markab*

Arabian syllables to Grecian myth,
the navel, shoulder, wing, and saddle back
of Pegasus, the fabled horse of heaven.

I close the book and step into the night,
the evening without moon, or cloud, and wait
to watch the constellation rise.
Up, up it comes, as it has ever come,
Between the Dolphin and Andromeda,
up, higher up, and swings into the clear.
And shall I say I hear the clang of hooves,
those silver hooves which stamped on Helicon
and struck forth Hippocrene, the Muses' spring?
And shall I say I see the quivering flank,
the wind swept mane, and feel the rhythmic stir
of white-spread wings fanning celestial space?
This would be Fancy's work, that tinsel tool
which bends and breaks upon reality.
The night is still, there is no silver clang,
no sound except the wind in stiffened leaves.
I see no winging horse, I only see
four wide-spaced, almost equidistant stars
which bound, unto this eye, a starless void.

The Square, majestic, moves to zenith height,
the old mythology grows meaningless.
Slowly new meaning comes, wordless at first,
the feeling of a bright security.
The Square, it is a Window! then I cry,
Casement secure against the endless dark.
And I rename the stars, and call them thus:
> *Pureness*   *Knowledge*
> *Reason*   *Love*
Window four-square unto the Infinite.
Nor is this Fancy. Neither bends nor breaks
upon reality that stronger tool
whose shining edge rings Nature into psalm.

I enter in the house and shut the door,
I will not watch the constellation set,
The Great Square shall not set! Experience,
the strongest tool, has carved it fixed. I look
within myself, steadfast the stars stand there.
The void they bound, O rich unfathomable!
Eternal workshop of the universe.
Therein lies Helicon and Hippocrene,
the crystal fount whose water quenches death;
therein amorphous chaos coils to form,
and speechless thought bespeaks the living word
whence cities, laws and industries arise.
There silence wells to music's overflow,
and filaments of feeling tendril Truth.
And there the primal Garden, cool and sweet,
offers its shade when man would walk with God.

EIGHT DOVES

Above the housetops eight doves fly,
And these eight doves can never die.

Now far apart, now close as one,
Eight pigeons circle in the sun;

They come to rest upon a roof,
And to the eight each one gives proof.

But when they wheel within the wide,
They neither add, nor yet divide;

They are not one, they are not eight,
They are this verse in which I state

That eight doves circle in the sun,
Now far apart, now close as one.

Theodore Dreiser

EVENING—MOUNTAINS

The shadowy hills
Aloud chant together
In audible crimson
The high-born peaks
Gleaming in the mournful redness
Of that madman's eye—
The sun—
Declare their defiance
Of their loneliness.
And about them,
In the steely desert of the sky
Wander cloud camels,
Red,
Slow,
And
In the valleys below
Under a twilight spell,
The earth itself
Enchanted
Rests.
And now
Some secret poet of the soul,
Finding this winding stream all black,
Flings upon its bosom
The poem of a star.

Estelle Duclo

O NATIONS!

O Nations! triumphant and vanquished, engrossed with
    your losses and gain,
The future, imperilled, is challenging you, through
    the voice of the slain!

Have you no statesman or soldier or poet or prophet
    to rise
With a saving and ultimate vision aflame in his kindled
    eyes?

Your counselors balance the fate of the world, while
    Time takes toll;—
Remember the scales of the spirit and their weighing
    of things of the soul.

Seek not the records of militant ages for guidance
    today,—
Let the sinister scrolls be annulled, let your wisdom
    and love lead the way.

The importunate hour awaits a word that shall quicken
    again,
The fires of faith and of courage and hope, in the hearts
    of men.

Mary Ballard Duryee

AND THE DAYS WERE ACCOMPLISHED

Now the bitter thorn has not
    Bloomed upon the bough
That will make a twisted crown
    For His holy brow;

Scarcely from the hidden seed
    Bursts the tender tree
To be hewn to shape a cross
    Raised on Calvary.

Now the hate that hung Him high
    Bides its certain hour,
While in youthful Pilate's dream
    Mercy strives with power.

Mary Cummings Eudy

OXEN

"Gee . . . Haw" . . . the furrow's deep,
And those who onward go must plod.
The day is long
And oxen have no song;
No sound is heard
Save "Gee . . . Haw!"
And curling lash
That cuts the raw
If step be taken wrong.

They know no plan
Of God or man,
Or how to weep;
They only know of furrows
Long . . . and . . . deep.

Rosemary Farrar

THE COCKS HAVE CROWED

Pale is the east with rising sun,
The cocks have crowed: and once again
Arrows of light will stab the lids
Of sleeping men.

In sooty flat on Depot Street,
In master room of fine estate,
The sleeping men will soon be waking—
Soon or late.

And they will yawn and curse the hour
And glancing at the world through slit
Of window, think how much they hate
The look of it.

Then, shaving at their mirrors, cracked
Or splendid, up and down the coast
Men will avoid the eyes of those
Who have betrayed them most.

Arthur Davison Ficke

LONG AND LOVELY

Long and lovely, cool and white,
She lay beside me all the night.

Long and lovely, hushed and warm,
She touched me, thigh and breast and arm.

My body was one tremulous sense
Of her slight body's eloquence.

I was a drowned man, in the sea
Of her immaculate melody.

Drifting slowly down to sleep,
I longed to laugh, I feared to weep.

While hushed and lovely, cool and white,
She lay beside me all the night.

Mahlon Leonard Fisher

WHEN I AM ENDED

When I am ended, and I see no more
The twilight take and crucify in flame
The Day that from an eastern manger came,
And seal his crypt with Shadow's blackest door,—
I would remember, underneath the floor
The flowers crowd upon, their loveliness;
And I would feel, in sleep, the plangent press

Of combers on the keyboards of the shore.
I would be cognizant of littlest things:
The cricket's iterance; and would hear, alone,
The luckless runlet stumbling over a stone;
And win, in vision, from that Spring of springs,
The ready nest, for birds which were to be,
Just caught between the fingers of a tree.

Kimball Flaccus

TO ALFRED KREYMBORG

A tree grows up by growing down . . .
Such nonsense might have made me frown
Four years ago, had I then heard
This strange distortion of the word,
This paradox elliptical,
Kreymborgian and cryptical.
So have I changed, I now admit
Paternity; I fathered it.
The phrase, in a symbolic way,
Expresses what I want to say.
Four years ago I thought you queer,—
German philosopher sans beer,
A clownish groom sans horse and carriage,
A non-conformist caught in marriage.
Lord knows how queer you must have thought me;
Perhaps the capitalists had bought me,
No doubt I was, to your shrewd eyes,
Young, and a great deal less than wise,
And vain and egotistical,
Impulsive, priggish, mystical.
Yet you were kind and you forbore,
And made me welcome at your door.

"Grow up! Grow up!" you might have cried,
"Send down your roots both deep and wide!"
For, nurtured by the academy,
In truth I was but half a tree.
Yet you were generous with your praise,
Disdained to wield the cutting phrase.
A radical I thought you then,
Embittered by the world of men;
A radical I think you now
But in a different sense somehow,—
Radical in the sense of root,
Fibre and earth and branch and fruit,
Sunlight and mineral salt and rain,
Structure that strengthens under strain.
Too many poets employ for theme
The half-tree image, pleasant dream
Of life as they wish life to be;
Blossom and leaf are all they see.
Events have hurtled on apace
Since first I met you face to face.
Now, having lived a little longer,
And, in the process, getting stronger,
And suffering more, seeing more clearly,
Loving humanity more dearly
With all its faults and all my own,
And claiming fellowship, blood and bone,
With every human on the earth,
I look back at my former dearth
And thank the friends who brought me through,—
This girl, that man, but mostly you.
Now, knowing you, I feel your warm
Humanity in a world of storm,
Admire the courage that lies behind
The whimsical surface of your mind.
For all your love, these draw your hate,—
Corruption in affairs of state,
Hypocrisy in any guise,
Expediency and compromise.

To oppose these things with tireless mettle
Is to invite a life-long battle;
To love humanity is to send
Graved summons to a Swiftian end,
Yet would I join you in the fight . . .
By growing down, a tree gains height.

John Gould Fletcher

RENEWAL TIME

The forests that were fired by men, return;
Out of their blackened stumps there springs forth many a seed:-
And the great wavering clouds of smoke that hung
Above them, now descend as rains to meet man's need.
The forests are renewed; and now the clock
That clocked the world's course, turns back to the hour
When all the trees that ever were, stood firm;
And the high wind, far-blowing, troubled not their power.

The animals come back, the panther first;
Who walked alone through the high desolate lands
And spread a legend of fear among the folk
Who first broke through the forest, in small bands.
The rest will follow; haughtily the deer
Lift up their heads and run. The porcupine
Goes sniffing for sweet globes where apples clung
To their abandoned branch. The others follow, in long line.

And people come too. Sometimes wandering far
Through the dark forest, we may find a friend
Or enemy of old gone under earth;
Such meetings shall the day after tomorrow send,
But these are ghosts; they will not speak to us,
Nor need we speak to them. Each goes his separate ways,

Not heeding much, nor over-curious,
In the long forest of forgotten yesterdays.

What of the flowers? Could they, too, rise again
When all this fire-wrecked forest is remade,
Or is there now for them, no still-renewing dawn
Down which the life-realm they could re-invade?
Clinging in drifts, like pale memorials
Of joys long past, I see them richlier burn,
And in strange forms complete the dream that glides
Through the long alleys of the sloping fern.

Ralph Friedrich

OF POEMS

Upon its shadowy edge
The forest of the mind
Conceals the wary hart,
Shelters the tremulous hind.

Such wonder burns upon
The ever-yearning sight
That the reluctant deer
Are stayed from needful flight.

But not the fiercest strength
Of all a man's desire
Can lure them into light,
However bright the fire

That burns in urgency
Along the forest's edge.
The darkness holds them fast;
No covenant or pledge

Persuades them to betray
Their fragile heritage.
A man is fortunate
If briefly on a page

Their shadows chance to fall
When suddenly upon
The forest ways they pass
And, star-like, yield to dawn.

Elizabeth Hollister Frost

DUST

I know a lady, (you know a lady),
    She is imbued with an ancient lust;
Not for gentlemen, not for shady
    Pools of lilies, but dust.

Now when the dream is on the slender
    Willow and lovers bruise the earth,
She is constrained with zeal to bend her
    Fingers to broom the hearth.

Save you, Lady, at your strange wooing,
    Stroke your broom with a tender thumb,
Whilst you consume sweet flesh pursuing
    The dust you'll soon become.

Robert Frost

A CONSIDERABLE SPECK
(*Microscopic*)

A speck that would have been beneath my sight
On any but a paper sheet so white
Set off across what I had written there.
And I had idly poised my pen in air
To stop it with a period of ink
When something strange about it made me think.
This was no dust speck by my breathing blown,
But unmistakably a living mite
With inclinations it could call its own.
It paused as with suspicion of my pen,
And then came racing wildly on again
To where my manuscript was not yet dry;
Then paused again and either drank or smelt—
With loathing, for again it turned to fly.
Plainly with an intelligence I dealt.
It seemed too tiny to have room for feet,
Yet must have had a set of them complete
To express how much it didn't want to die.
It ran with terror and with cunning crept.
It faltered: I could see it hesitate;
Then in the middle of the open sheet
Cower down in desperation to accept
Whatever I accorded it of fate.

I have none of the tenderer-than-thou
Collectivistic regimenting love
With which the modern world is being swept.
But this poor microscopic item now!
Since it was nothing I knew evil of
I let it lie there till I hope it slept.

I have a mind myself and recognize
Mind when I meet with it in any guise.
No one can know how glad I am to find
On any sheet the least display of mind.

THE MOST OF IT

He thought he kept the universe alone;
For all the voice in answer he could wake
Was but the mocking echo of his own
From some tree-hidden cliff across the lake.
Some morning from the boulder-broken beach
He would cry out on life, that what it wants
Is not its own love back in copy speech,
But counter-love, original response.
And nothing ever came of what he cried
Unless it was the embodiment that crashed
In the cliff's talus on the other side,
And then in the far distant water splashed,
But after a time allowed for it to swim,
Instead of proving human when it neared
And someone else additional to him,
As a great buck it powerfully appeared,
Pushing the crumpled water up ahead,
And landed pouring like a waterfall,
And stumbled through the rocks with horny tread,
And faced the underbrush—and that was all.

COME IN

As I came to the edge of the woods,
Thrush music—hark!
Now if it was dusk outside,
Inside it was dark.

Too dark in the woods for a bird
By sleight of wing
To better its perch for the night,
Though it still could sing.

The last of the light of the sun
That had died in the west
Still lived for one song more
In a thrush's breast.

Far in the pillared dark
Thrush music went—
Almost like a call to come in
To the dark and lament.

But no, I was out for stars:
I would not come in.
I meant not even if asked,
And I hadn't been.

Ethel Romig Fuller

THE DARK CHAMBER

Within an orbit of aloofness, each
Life spins, nor touches but the outer sphere
Of planetary bodies whirling near—
A firmament of selves, beyond the reach
Of closer contact than abrasive speech,
Which mars the patina, but leaves the pith
As nebulous as truth sought in a myth;
Secretive as the stone heart of a peach.

More desolate than virgin Everest:
White mystery behind a monsoon's hood—
The dark inviolate chamber of the breast
Where dreams are domiciled, and sorrows brood;
More lone, more inaccessible than are
The unexplored blue frontiers on a star.

Theodosia Garrison

STAINS

The three ghosts on the lonesome road
    Spake each to one another,
"Whence came that stain about your mouth
    No lifted hand may cover?"
"From eating of forbidden fruit,
    Brother, my brother."

The three ghosts on the sunless road
    Spake each to one another,
"Whence came that red burn on your foot
    No dust nor ash may cover?"
"I stamped a neighbor's hearth-flame out,
    Brother, my brother."

The three ghosts on the windless road
    Spake each to one another,
"Whence came that blood upon your hand
    No other hand may cover?"
"From breaking of a woman's heart,
    Brother, my brother."

"Yet on the earth clean men we walked,
    Glutton and Thief and Lover;
White flesh and fair it hid our stains
    That no man might discover."
"Naked the soul goes up to God,
    Brother, my brother."

Minna Gellert

TRANSLATION FROM A LOST LANGUAGE

During the high noon of time,
The fullest hour, the most transitory
When proof was wedded to the dream,
A glass-blower, in a trance of joy,
From liquid space designed a bell
To chime in crystal.
On fluid sound he placed his hand
To give the perfect hour tongue,
And mournfully the twelve notes rang
As though a swan had sung.

FLESH OF THE FURIES

Each of my mothers was beautiful,
They spoke together
In seven languages of silence,
Among them they built a multiple destiny.

But I was lured by the staring eye;
I rode the sleeping stallion of folly
Bareback in moonlight,
Unburdened of twenty years of wisdom—
My mothers wept.

After a thousand nightmares
I dream it still,
The marble flower that bleeds and bleeds,
Growing from my skeleton
The color of ambushed fear,
The stern petals of perfection
Destroying the stem.

There is always moonlight and the rider
Naked under the shadow of his innocence,

Hoofs churning the marble flowers
And the sterile, exciting taste of sand.

Each of my mothers was beautiful,
They spoke together
In seven languages of silence,
Among them they built a multiple destiny.

Clifford Gessler

SIESTA HOUR

The heavy hand of afternoon weighs down
upon the dampened forehead of the town.
The island city sleeps: its tranquil dust
inscribed with devious, obscure signatures
of silent wheels, its piety and lust
alike held netted in the filatures
of heat. The roofs, like sleek and drowsy cats,
bask in the sunlight, and the plaited mats
are ports for fragile cargo-fleets of dreams.
    Only the coco-palm is wakeful there,
tossing its tawny mane in flashing beams
of challenge to vanilla-drunken air.
        So the heart sleeps, in its due season, making
        a secret rendezvous for its awaking.

Kahlil Gibran

LOVE

They say the jackal and the mole
Drink from the self-same stream
Where the lion comes to drink.

And they say the eagle and the vulture
Dig their beaks into the same carcass,
And are at peace, one with the other,
In the presence of the dead thing.

O love, whose lordly hand
Has bridled my desires,
And raised my hunger and my thirst
To dignity and pride,
Let not the strong in me and the constant
Eat the bread or drink the wine
That tempt my weaker self.
Let me rather starve,
And let my heart parch with thirst,
And let me die and perish,
Ere I stretch my hand
To a cup you did not fill,
Or a bowl you did not bless.

Yetza Gillespie

BLUE HERON

Here, here among the reeds he stands,
Where shallows meet the shore,
As stark as stone, aloof as time,
Oblivious of my oar.

So unexpected of each other,
So suddenly so near,
The feral and the human eyes
Renounce the veil of fear.

Woman and bird entranced, we stare
Till grass and water seem
A rippled world, a memory,
The nebulae of dream.

And we are legendary, bound
With a chain of fabled links,
Papyrus figures pondering
The riddle of the Sphynx . . .

The moment opens. He is gone,—
A slanting maltese line,—
Seeking his dinner. I am I
Again, in search of mine.

Louis Ginsberg

WHEN BOMBS ON BARCELONA BURST

When bombs on Barcelona burst,
    I was a thousand miles away;
And yet my walls cracked wide apart
    And fell on me in disarray.

It was not so much splintering
    Of glass on my once sheltered place,
As ominous and crackling sounds
    Of justice broken on my face.

My room can never be repaired,
    Until there is atonement first,
For those who died, because I slept,
    When bombs on Barcelona burst.

Mae Winkler Goodman

EMILY DICKINSON

She spoke the dialect of birds,
    The synonym of bees;
She paraphrased a morning dew,
    And gossiped with a breeze.

The Mediterranean licked her shoe,
    The Alps she reckoned friends;
At home on Iceland's barren shore,
    Or in Saraha's sands,

She never went to seek the world,
   Yet spied it at her feet,
And trespassed through eternity
   Down a New England street.

William Griffith

PIERRETTE IN MEMORY

Pierrette has gone, but it was not
   Exactly that she died
So much as vanished and forgot
   To say where she would hide.

To keep a sudden rendezvous,
   It came into her mind
That she was late. What could she do
   But leave distress behind?

Afraid of being in disgrace,
   And hurrying to dress,
She heard there was another place
   In need of loveliness.

She went so softly and so soon—
   She hardly made a stir;
But going took the stars and moon
   And sun away with her.

Louise Imogen Guiney

IRISH PEASANT SONG

I try to knead and spin, but my life is low the while.
Oh, I long to be alone, and walk abroad a mile;
Yet if I walk alone, and think of naught at all,
Why from me that's young should the wild tears fall?

The shower-sodden earth, the earth-colored streams,
They breathe on me awake, and moan to me in dreams,
And yonder ivy fondling the broke castle-wall,
It pulls upon my heart till the wild tears fall.

The cabin-door looks down a furze-lighted hill,
And far as Leighlin Cross the fields are green and still;
But once I hear the blackbird in Leighlin hedges call,
The foolishness is on me, and the wild tears fall!

Arthur Guiterman

ON THE VANITY OF EARTHLY GREATNESS

The tusks that clashed in mighty brawls
Of mastodons are billiard balls.

The sword of Charlemagne the Just
Is ferric oxide, known as rust.

The grizzly bear whose potent hug
Was feared by all is now a rug.

Great Caesar's bust is on the shelf,
And I don't feel so well myself.

Ralph Gustafson

ON THE STRUMA MASSACRE

Now as these slaughtered seven hundreds hear
The vulgar sennet of thine angel sound,
Grant, in thy love, that they may see that ground
Whose promised acres holy footsteps bear.
For they of only this made credulous prayer—
Even for whom thy Son the tempest bound
And waters walked O not those same where, drowned,
Driven by plausible tongues and mute despair,
These faithful roll! No not as they, with board
And spike, who took Thy sweetness then, do we—
Studied in ignorance, and knowing Thee.
For Thine archaic crown of thorns and cord,
Statistics are become Thine agony,
The ocean designate, Gabbatha, Lord.

FLIGHT INTO DARKNESS

We have fulfilled our apprehension, hope,
Matched our hands' delay against the sun,
Against a guttering candle written dreams.
Was it today we fumbled spiral of spring,
Clutched at the throat the knot of accurate winds.
Noose and thong by beauty slung?

Yesterday yesterday! the hills were bare of snow,
The hackneyed maple broke with leaf, the bough
Sprang colour along the sweetened air—whose action
Pledged our anger. O we have sworn our lives
Between the hyphened prologue of the crow,
The crimson coming of the rose!

Who now, regretting June with adult smiles,
Set nodding with a finger Buddha's porcelain head:

Hearing of marvels in the township, turned
Expensive keys against the empty street,
From possible cars saw moon eclipse the sun,
Cautious glass before our eyes.

And all that year the tamarack was green
And we who saw the tolerant seed and snow,
By leaning questions ambushed. Grace was then
The grateful turning-out of lamps at night,
Within the book the treacherous flower's clue,
The short escape of perjured love.

For we remembering our defence refused
The mirror's prosecution, praised the speaker
On the chairman's right: within the files,
Found brief anger for the anonymous clock,
Looking up, the calendar on startled walls—
Withdrawing truth from blundering sleep.

We have waited important letters from the west,
In evening cities heard the newspaper tossed
Against the door, under the prosperous valley
Guessed at oil, proved the legend false.
We dream wisely who once had loved too well.
And yet, coming on sun across

An alien street, stand suddenly surprised—
As Galileo, before his midnight window,
Cloak about his shoulders, coldly chose
A fatal planet—first, listened while
The solitary wagon passed along the road—
Then aimed his contradictory lens.

Hermann Hagedorn

DOORS

Like a young child who to his mother's door
    Runs eager for the welcoming embrace,
    And finds the door shut, and with troubled face
Calls and through sobbing calls, and o'er and o'er
Calling, storms at the panel—so before
    A door that will not open, sick and numb,
    I listen for a word that will not come,
And know, at last, I may not enter more.

Silence! And through the silence and the dark
    By that closed door, the distant sob of tears
    Beats on my spirit, as on fairy shores
The spectral sea; and through the sobbing—hark!
    Down the fair-chambered corridor of years,
    The quiet shutting, one by one, of doors.

Amanda Benjamin Hall

THE SCHOOL BOY LEARNS TO FLY

He craves a bird's career—
Do not dissuade him!
Without the flaw of fear
The Lord has made him,
Whom words of caution tend
To make the sadder . . .
O, watch him now ascend
The rungless ladder!

To-day he does not pore
Over a book. Blood courses
Through his veins—this lore
Is learned from higher sources;
From winds that sing and talk
He gleans a bird's own culture—
Behold the gentle hawk,
The innocent vulture!

INSTANT OUT OF TIME

All day the moments gathered for the moment
When he must go. The clock's face, strange, unkind,
Seemed flushed with speed; the great hand spun the circle,
The lesser hand was never far behind!

Until the hour was screwed in place forever . . .
Then, with a trembling of its inner parts,
The time-piece spoke. The tolling sound was ruthless
To halt the conversation of our hearts . . .

Long since I've set my barren house in order
And tidied up my wild, dishevelled pain;
The breathless clock has no more need to hurry—
The days have back their leisure once again.

Though gone in truth, forever he goes from me,
Swift with the clear compulsion of a brook,
Across his shoulder giving me one final
                    Enormous look!

Hazel Hall

TWO SEWING

The wind is sewing with needles of rain;
With shining needles of rain
It stitches into the thin
Cloth of earth—in,
In, in, in.
Oh, the wind has often sewed with me!—
One, two, three.

Spring must have fine things
To wear, like other springs.
Of silken green the grass must be
Embroidered. *One and two and three.*
Then every crocus must be made
So subtly as to seem afraid
Of lifting color from the ground;
And after crocuses the round
Heads of tulips, and all the fair
Intricate garb that Spring will wear.
The wind must sew with needles of rain,
With shining needles of rain
Stitching itno the thin
Cloth of earth—in,
In, in, in—
For all the springs of futurity.
One, two, three.

Marion Ethel Hamilton

CHILDREN ON A HILL

I heard a sound of voices from the hill
All through the afternoon, and children calling;
Some unborn Rover romped and barked, I felt
Them playing there until the dusk was falling.

I heard their voices, fainter, float away
As they went homeward down the darkening hill;
These sweet immortal children, forever at play;
These pale immortal children, forever still.

Leigh Hanes

SCREECH OWLS

Once every summer, in an emerald light,
I watch the little screech owls try their wings
For the first time, between the dusk and night
    Eerie with quaverings.

But whence they come I never yet have known,
Save that the woods seem full of owlet doors,
And come they do, ubiquitously blown
    In two's and three's and four's,

Till suddenly I have become aware
Of wizened faces, cowled heads awry,
And eyes that stare as only owlets stare
    Before they tilt and fly:

Leaving me there in darkness to surmise
How well it goes with owlets in their flight,
And silent wings, and fixed nocturnal eyes
    Needing no outer light.

MOON MAGIC

Strange, how the moon will come
Full from the breast of trees,
Rubbing soft fingers and thumb
On silvery keys;

Stand at a door made fast,
Call not a name nor knock,
Find the worn key at last,
Turn the hushed lock,—

Enter, and fumble around
Touching a gown or a face,
Leave without taking a sound
Out of the place.

Elizabeth Stanton Hardy

THE ARISTOCRAT

From the taut hills, the austere pine
Rooted in rigid soil; from rock
Of hard and unrelenting line
Comes bone of his New England stock.

Mixed with the lime of fossil beaches,
Where ocean combs the truant shells;
Chastened by the white steepled reaches
Of multitudinous Sabbath bells.

And once this virtue turns the blood,
Always upon a changing planet
He will be prisoner root and bud,
Of something definite as granite.

As if upon an island born
With boundaries drawn, surrounded,—then
His firm and fine estate will scorn
The mainlands of inconsequent men.

SIGNATURE UPON ROCK

What years of slow erosion, tide and ice
Channeled across this ante-glacial stone!
What eons ground, minutely and precise
The drift of stardust into flesh and bone.

Centuries hence some paleontologist will
Pick this proud civilization like a lock,
And say, 'From mollusk stemmed the race, until
There spawned this strange breed kenneled in the rock.

'They lived a million chiliads ago,
After the Java man, the Piltdown branch;
Leaving clean cut, a chaste intaglio
Under the shale and granite avalanche.'

'Pointed with haste, look, how a rush of feet
Have left their print. What hunger drove these men?
See how these footsteps climb a fossil street
Only to turn and hurry back again.'

Amory Hare

THE CROWN

Thrice have I seemed to view Eternity.
The night my first-born leapt against my side;
Once when I cried
To God and watched a star fall down the sky,
Flung earthward for my lonely soul's reprieve;
And once when, quietly,
You laid your tired hands upon my head
And smiling said
'Believe'.

Gwendolen Haste

DEATH OF THE GRANDMOTHER

It is almost forgotten . . . the stepping down from swinging light
To the night crossed by the shape of trees; grumble of motion
And the smell of horses, dull penumbras of light and tall
    blackness.
There is no home in these streets, only recollections of odor,
    light,
Motion, from days when things broke in the mind to foaming
    outlines.
Far back in the sleepy brain a faintly known remembering
Swings with the creak of the omnibus and iron shoes on brick
    pavement.

There is a return through saved memories to the slippered
    scuffle.

Long since the large grace of the Persian lilac was old with the
grapevine
Bending on its trellis. Ponies that once stamped in the barn
Died long ago; ridden no more by girls now lost in taffeta
And emerald-glinting hands, passing the frail cup,
Tipping the brass shine above the spirit lamp.
Go back . . . renew yourself in these colored wells.

Lamps shed paleness spilling on dark cupboards, painted glass
doors
Holding all that has gone. The catalpas have dropped green
pencils
Now dry patterned brown on cold lawn. Nothing is left of the
peonies
But a round death. As sleep curtains the mind there are bells,
Minor clangings that fall through the catalpa boughs . . .
The whistle at crossing . . . the muffled voice of the shunting . . .
Dreams in this strange yet remembered house circled by bells.

For the young the old die with ease, a ceasing in quiet of one
Who was kind hands. Too early to learn death. The habit
Of funeral strikes queerly . . . a loss not felt but remembered
in pictures
Crude with infancy, before that face had changed to the remote
glance
From the sheet or the voice was stilled by the death-coming.
Pictures that lie
In the remembering mind while the eyes watch an old man lost
in deafness
And grief who speaks of a past known only to the blood not the
memory.

April, and nothing will hinder the catalpa from urging her rich
blossom,
Nor will the blue grape ever cease, and the locust
Over the herringbone drive has an eternity with the house.
Only years will mix shingles and graceful dish, the catalpa and
the clap of hooves

And the sad harmony of the bells with this dead who returns
    diffidently
In dream to a home romantically enlarged by dreaming . . .
Rooms sheathed in walnut . . . halls singular with shadow . . .

Where the dreamer walks certain of destination, lighting
Her rapid journey with bobbing candle through rooms and
    stairs
Brought into night-dark being by that light, reflecting now
The panel shine of a closed alcove bed where dreams say
Lie those two so long past dreaming, now sleeping as they rested
In that time behind a closed green-painted door
Where a child might tiptoe not disturbing the fluid slumber
    of old age.

There lies in the mind as that dream lay in sleep, the jewel of
    the beginnings,
That which is ancestral, curtained by the catalpa, the high swell
    of the locust,
And the tune of the circling bells. Rejoice it shall never be lost,
For losing it life would be a faint thing shuddering vainly in
    the day.

OPHIDIA

Lifting dark beside the trail
Blotched by the pale
'Sunlight sifting through cedars;
Mark of beast, stir of bee,
But here no least foot of man has beaten track,
And the traveler shudders back
From the narrow needled floor.
This is a door into legend.
Tales of men caught among patterned horror,
Beside caverns painted with sun,
With clubbed gun a slack weapon
Rasping a last breath
In swollen death.

Let the mild cedars roar
Over the cushioned floor
While the tales pour
Down the wind from that place of bright caverns,
Down paths known only to wild feet and the dead—
The dread touch of life that lies in the sunlight alone
Warm on a stone.

Fanny de Groot Hastings

CORAL LIZARD

How has the dragon shrunken in this age!
The foe of Michael's sword, St. George's rage
And Arthur's chivalry, the sire
Of legendary monsters, breathing fire,
Half lion and half serpent, has become
A small and harmless lizard, shy and dumb.
This kin of ancient terror-striking beasts
Measures a finger's length and gladly feasts
On gnats unworthy a bird's appetite.
Now gracefully it glides out of the light,
Its coat, the tint of coral bells in flower,
Brightened by dews that are its daily shower—
A timid creature entering its lair
All overhung with tender maidenhair.

Sara Henderson Hay

THE BEASTS

"And the beasts of the field shall be at peace with thee . . ."
                                                    Job 5, 23.

Oh think—the satin-skinned, the dapple,
The doe with her fawn,
Standing at gaze, calm-eyed, untroubled,
Their terror gone.

Think—the round rabbit, the plumed squirrel,
The lynx, too,
And the wolf, forgetful of his quarrel,
With man, with you.

Even the curved panther, he
With knives along his jaw—
How soft his heavy head upon your knee,
And his furled paw!

CHILD ON THE BEACH

Here at the edge of foam I watch him stand,
This child made pygmy by the sky and sea,
Clutching a pebble in his small square hand,
His little charm against infinity.
"It is my magic stone," he says to me,
Absurd and innocent. With heart and mind
I ponder his magician's game, and he
Is suddenly the symbol of his kind . . .

Man, strutting childlike on a wider shore,
Facing a tide more resolutely sweeping
Beyond the moon of his brief sky's control.
As confident, as vulnerable before
A fathomless oblivion, and keeping
Tight in his hand the pebble of his soul.

Daniel Henderson

CONSIDER, LORD, OUR CLERK

Consider, Lord, our clerk.
In shimmering array
She came to morning work—
Oh precious Saturday!
Now all her tasks are done—
And Jerry calls at one.

See—at the window-pane,
She frowns with Sue and Jane.
These dark and sudden clouds
Put her bright hopes in shrouds—
For oh, so brief is Sunday,
And oh, the time-clock Monday!

Yes, there is need of showers,
But ere it is too late—
Just for the next few hours,
Lord, let her keep her date.
For this one day in seven,
Please give her a blue heaven!

DuBose Heyward

THE MOUNTAIN WOMAN

Among the sullen peaks she stood at bay
And paid life's hard account from her small store.
Knowing the code of mountain wives, she bore
The burden of the days without a sigh;

And, sharp against the somber winter sky,
I saw her drive her steers afield each day.

Hers was the hand that sunk the furrows deep
Across the rocky, grudging southern slope.
At first youth left her face, and later hope;
Yet through each mocking spring and barren fall,
She reared her lusty brood, and gave them all
That gladder wives and mothers love to keep.

And when the sheriff shot her eldest son
Beside his still, so well she knew her part,
She gave no healing tears to ease her heart;
But took the blow upstanding, with her eyes
As drear and bitter as the winter skies.
Seeing her then, I thought that she had won.

But yesterday her man returned too soon
And found her tending, with a reverent touch,
One scarlet bloom; and, having drunk too much,
He snatched its flame and quenched it in the dirt.
Then, like a creature with a mortal hurt,
She fell, and wept away the afternoon.

Sophie Himmell

SLEEP

Scoop a handful of night,
Scoop it deep,
Lay it across your eyes,
Fall into sleep—

Fall till you lose
The sight of the sun,

Fall till you reach
.Oblivion.

I know no other
Cure for pain;
Borrowed joy
Bewilders the brain,

Borrowed ease
Bedevils the mind;
Lay night on your eyes
Till you are blind—

Till the pain is gone
Like an autumn leaf:
I know no other
Cure for grief.

Dorothy Hobson

AWAKENING

Come, let us sell the past and future, giving
The proceeds to the poor: see, here is living,
Here is the now of living, tingling, tart;
Let us have done with counting memories,
With huddling over blueprints, let us have done
With polishing the furniture of the heart
And all the mind's inane housewiferies
Amid the cluttered yesterdays and tomorrows.
Let us have done at last with saving sorrows,
With turning into salt or worrying forward.

Let us rub our eyes and stretch like risen men;
Let us look up for once, and out again,

Up to the sky, the sun, out here to where
The moments are, the live and moving air,
The delicate blow upon the naked sense,
Tang, taste, sound and flavor, the present tense,
The savoring of breath's immediate plunder,
Stinging us far too wide awake to say
That was the time, or *That will be the day,*
Or anything but: *This is the now of wonder.*

Marcia Nichols Holden

CONVENT

Minutes were poplars on the avenue
And a nun gliding, feet unseen, down corridor
Jet rosary beads clicking on a crucifix
Her greeting soft as cotton in the ears.

Time was homesickness.
The last piece of chocolate
Regulation black garb
White veils on Sundays and Feast Days
And chapelled nights
Sharp as apples in fall orchards.

Then time was ice on a flooded tennis court
Snow under a toboggan
The ski jump

And embroidered patience
The long thread, the lazy worker.
Scott's Emulsion on the sideboard of the refectory
Sulphured molasses.

Always prayers
Like the crocused Shrine in the woods
Or a Passion Play
(Sky rent with piano thunder and a quick hand on the light
    switch)
Purple in the Chapel
The three hour silence.

Until morning's rhubarbed taste
Warmed for a nested robin
And squeaking oar-locks on the squared artificial lake
Mixed with the soaped smell from the laundry on fine days.

Memories going out under the arch of the Cross
In colored dresses.

Raymond Holden

THE MIND HAS STUDIED FLIGHT

Against the sky a sea bird's breast of cloud,
Against the cloud a true gull and his curve.
Against the rock a tress of kelp and, loud
Among the crevices, the pulse and nerve
Of a sea quickening to moon and wind.
Here by the sea the trouble in the heart
Matches the unequal trouble of the mind—
Judgment and joy at war and far apart.
Down swoops the strong, spray-colored, sea-soft bird
Upon his fish, without "ought-not" or "ought."
Man, flightless master of the flying word,
Follows his every act with afterthought.
And yet a man, whose conscience is his wing

And must be tilted to the carrying air
Of that sphere marked for wit's inhabiting,
Looks at the gulls and knows what keeps them there.

Thought, like a bird, is mannerless and swift
To snatch for substance at the hollow tide
Where those effects and promised actions drift
Which keep the fed thing on the living side.
Balanced within its element, the mind
Has studied flight. Even to the carrion gull
It is akin, even to his crying kind.
Now the mind's man, in this cool evening's lull
Of wind and light looks out to sea and hears
The sheaves of water shifting on the rock,
The sea bird's wailing waving at his ears,
The heartbeat in his side saying "knock," saying "knock."

AWAKE UNDER STARS

O pitiful and unprotected mind
Guilty of such confusion and such waste
That even your housing breast and skull are laced
With blood of terror, did you think to find
For punishment, dismissal everywhere,
Proud stars arranging to arrest their courses
And fall upon your head like hooves of horses?
And what are you that men and heaven should care?
The child that childhood lay in wait to kill
Bears flower often; and the spendthrift wealth,
Awkwardness beauty, ill condition health.
You are a child, a spendthrift, awkward, ill.
Look up and see that, even after all,
The star you feared still has all heaven to fall.

Frances Minturn Howard

FOUNDATION

Beneath the flow of words
Light as lifted hair
Colored by the sun,
Articulate with air,

There moves the bone of thought,
Socketed and clear,
On its fine-tooled joint
White, remote, austere.

Delight who will the smooth
Artifice of tongue,
The silver-bodied core
On which the flesh is hung,

Is sweeter to the eye
That sees the naked skull
Luminous beneath
And knows it beautiful.

MARTYR

Beware this man who carries in
His breast the fagots that shall turn
His little bones to curling ash;
Himself this man shall burn.

Avoid his table, where are served
The stones that are his daily bread;
This is a curious board he keeps;
A skull sits at the head.

The fluid element that wears
His flesh, more violent than kind,

Shakes off the fragile body-stuff
From the harder mind,

And he shall move the rooted hills
And make the rocks articulate,
And tear the rivers from their beds
To come upon his fate.

Dorothy Berry Hughes

THE HAND

Now lay the hand along the folds of rest,
Light as a petal, cool, inert. The day
Is stored, the sum of it, for here is pressed
The elaborate intaglio of steel;
The mute experience of touch that lies
Beyond the subtle ear, beyond the eyes,
Leaves in the memory, half dream, half real,
The tracery of love, and anger's way,
The ample tool, and craft, and beauty done:
Will and resistant earth, spirit and stone.

Josephine Jacobsen

FOR A DANCER

Paint bites deep
And will last your day
And then beyond it, a century.

Marble will stop,
When empires burn;
It will wait in the ground the cold spade's turn.

What melody
Is kin to the flesh?
It is yours no more than a wind or a wish.

But this has the mark
Of such as we;
This is the art of mortality.

This is our own
As never another;
The link of the stone and the note with the feather.

Ancient and true—
But weightless as foam,
And gone with the dancer as heat with the flame.

MIDNIGHT EDEN

The crusted Tree of stars soars quite
Across the sky,
Mammoth, unstirred, stiff with a bright
Rigidity.

The branches glitter, forked and still
In the great air,
Distant, enormous; by midnight visible
And very fair.

The Tree, the Tree, lovely, and not for us;
With light for wood
It grows, as ever, desired, dangerous,
Not understood.

Leslie Nelson Jennings

CARPENTRY

Hour after hour, deliberate stroke on stroke,
The hammer kept on beating its busy tune,
Until the insistent rhythm of it broke
Into my dream. I looked and saw the moon
Was waning over towns that slept content
In a cool, paling darkness, but I rose,
Breathing an air withheld—I rose and went
Softly as wind along a river goes.

Who toiled away the night so full of zeal?
There were no stars hung out above my quest;
Silence came after like a hound at heel—
Only the moon went staggering down the west.
And then day broke . . . O Carpenter, for whom
Do you build houses of a single room?

Orrick Johns

TREE TOAD

A tiny bell the tree toad has,
    I wonder if he knows
The charm it is to hear him,
    Ringing as he goes.

He can't have gone the journeys
    He tells me to go on,
Here in the darkness
    Of the cool, cropped lawn.

He cannot know the thrill
    Of the soft spring wind,
Or the wonder when you walk,
    What will come behind.

He hasn't seen the places
    I'd break my heart to win,
Nor heard the city calling
    When the cold comes in.

He sings away contented,
    And doesn't leave his tree,
But he sets my blood a-going
    Where his song will never be.

WILD PLUM

They are unholy who are born
    To love wild plum at night,
Who once have passed it on a road
    Glimmering and white.

It is as though the darkness had
    Speech of silver words,
Or as though a cloud of stars
    Perched like ghostly birds.

They are unpitied from their birth
    And homeless in men's sight
Who love, better than the earth,
    Wild plum at night.

Josephine Johnson

LOW COUNTRY

Ever the ocean tides, slipping between the islands,
Shaking the piers, shaking the old palmetto
posts where the barnacles cling—
leaving a scrawl on the beaches, leaving the bright staccato
scuttling of crabs. Turning again to swing
out through the shoal-green reaches.

Islands lying like fruit, strewn out beyond the shoreline,
fruit of the sea—softly bloomed with sea-cotton,
husked with saw grass—pale in the noonday glimmer
shimmer in indolent beauty, still as the strong are still;
savage at heart, intent on a primal will,
deaf to entreaty.

Mosses drip from the trees. Embraces of greybeards
would strangle the surgent green where pine and juniper rip
through tangles of vine and creeper. Live oaks stir,
shake their great limbs, and the air is spattered with light
as a swimmer scatters bright drops. The cypress, at ease,
hunches his bony knees in the dark swamp water.

Fecund and beautiful land! Tenacious, intent, and sufficing,
where life flows on in a rhythm of tides and seasons,
what do they know of death when the gulf winds rising
fumble along these coasts, and the turtle stumbles
heavy with eggs, while out of his ghostly skin
the moccasin ripples, thin as a damask blade?

The altar may lie untended, the censer broken,
the ritual lost—but ever the estuary
throbs with an ageless pulse. In the heart of the swamp
life is burning and wary. April has spoken.

Churning his foaming ring
out of the reeking damp the bull alligator
bellows of spring!

Victoria Saffelle Johnson

THE GREAT BLUE HERON

Where Sanderlings, like children, run
Behind the wet, receding tide,
And Killdeer greet the morning sun
Above the sandy oceanside,
The Great Blue Herons slowly stalk
With heavy purpose in their walk.

While little Snowy Plover play
Along the stretch of quiet sand,
And sea gulls laugh above the bay
Or chuckle harshly from the land,
The Herons, with no thought of mirth,
Stand contemplating heaven and earth.

All day upon the beach they wait
To pounce and feed, as Herons must,
On drowsy fish that wake too late
To flee the watchers' deadly thrust.
While neighbors wander wide and free,
The Herons stand to watch the sea.

Leila Jones

LOCKET FOR THE HEART

Nail moonlight to the bark of cherry;
Hide the gold fan of wind that blows
The banished leaf; the wild white berry
That stares across the autumn snows.

Hoard the blue husks of waxen seed
Strung on a thread, so late to fall;
The harlequin paint of jewel-weed
That droops a bauble on the wall.

These for the traveller that makes
Winter his way, to succor him;
More in the hand than honey-cakes
Or wine to stain a tankard's brim.

He bears a keepsake in his pack
For summer spent and autumn lost,
When every tree is powder-black,
And every meadow stark with frost.

Mary Hoxie Jones

HARVEST

("*There will be no war until men have been able to harvest
their crops.*" *1938*)

Now are the crops
    Stored safely away.

Barley and hops,
  Potatoes and hay.

Let the winds blow
  Cold from the north.
Let the men go,
  Marshall them forth.

Now let them die
  For glory of God.
Safe let them lie
  Under the sod.

Empty their veins,
  Strangle their breath.
All that remains
  Living is death.

Wheat has been ground
  To flour for bread.
Who shall be found?
  Who shall be fed?

Now are the crops
  Rotting away.
Mould in the hops,
  Rust in the hay.

Rats gnaw the wheat,
  Worms eat the dead.
War will defeat
  Even man's bread.

Ruth Lambert Jones

PREVISION

I will cross that bridge
Before I come to it.
How else shall I find
The sea
And the lean gray masts
And the wheeling sails
Of my necessity!
I will cross that bridge
Before I come to it.
Do not follow me.

Thomas S. Jones, Jr.

CLONMACNOISE

No autumn woods have wreathed with deepest red
    The god-like conquerors that sleep uncrowned
    In riven tumulus and ruined mound,
Their mighty deeds by time discredited;
No vineyard pall of purpling gold is spread
    Above the Fenian hunter and his hound,
    Or saint who waits an angel's horn unwound
Across the lonely meadows of the dead.

But one last Hero holds the wasted field,
    Whose fallen greatness makes all triumph vain
By memory of a sepulchre unsealed;

And still one reaper waits by Ciaran's plain
To take his tithe of sheaves, where shield on shield
Earth's golden kings are strewn like garnered grain.

Hannah Kahn

NO MORE POEMS

I always wanted to make up poems
but they always got me in trouble.

When I started to work at the Savoy Restaurant
I waited on a lady
who had a dress with red hearts embroidered all over it
and I started to make up a poem
about the ladies who wore embroidered hearts
on their dresses
and the bleeding hearts we used to have
in our yard.
When the poem began to move around in my head,
I dropped the tray
and spilled coffee on the lady with the embroidered hearts.

She made a big rumpus and told the manager on me
and I got fired.

But I wasn't even going to look for another job.
I had a hundred and eighty-six dollars saved up
and I thought the time was here when I
could write.

I wanted to make up poems
about the old men who looked at the dinner menu
for a long time
and then ordered doughnuts and coffee.

And I was going to write about
a lot of other kinds of people too.

But as soon as I had time
it looked like I had nothing to write about
and it looked so unnecessary to try to say it

so I called up the manager of the Savoy
and we went to Coney Island on Sunday
and I'm working at the Savoy again.

Lucy Kent

WINTER OVERTURE

We walk into the wide embrace
Of autumn
Where desire has an old face
And the hands of the year
Drop from the trees
Wrinkled and sear.

Fragments of summer
Crushed by the heel,
The leaf and the fallen feather,
Lie voiceless on the ground
Like part of a broken wheel,
A shattered souvenir,
Only the heart can hold together.

This is the hour
Most empty, most still,
When only the rock and the hill
And the naked trembling tree
Answer serenity.

This is the hour
When every heart is most alone
Hearing the tall trees bend
And the wind's descriptive moan;

Here in this hour
When summer lies mute
In the perpetual root
Only grief is awake
To watch the wind shake,
Down from the sky's expanse,
The snow's first delicate flake.

Aline Kilmer

MY MIRROR

There is a mirror in my room
Less like a mirror than a tomb,
There are so many ghosts that pass
Across the surface of the glass.

When in the morning I arise
With circles round my tired eyes,
Seeking the glass to brush my hair,
My mother's mother meets me there.

If in the middle of the day
I happen to go by that way,
I see a smile I used to know—
My mother, twenty years ago.

But when I rise by candlelight
To feed my baby in the night,
Then whitely in the glass I see
My dead child's face look out at me.

Joyce Kilmer

PRAYER OF A SOLDIER IN FRANCE

My shoulders ache beneath my pack
(Lie easier, Cross, upon His back).

I march with feet that burn and smart
(Tread, Holy Feet, upon my heart).

Men shout at me who may not speak
(They scourged Thy back and smote Thy cheek).

I may not lift a hand to clear
My eyes of salty drops that sear.

(Then shall my fickle soul forget
Thy Agony of Bloody Sweat?)

My rifle hand is stiff and numb
(From Thy pierced palm red rivers come).

Lord, Thou didst suffer more for me
Than all the hosts of land and sea.

So let me render back again
This millionth of Thy gift. Amen.

Sally Bruce Kinsolving

GO DOWN, MOSES

Long have I heard the rhythm of the sea
Swinging her silver tides on moonlit sands
Or throbbing with the soul of many lands,
Great orchestras in measured unity.
But here at last I know that I have found
In swelling surge, in rhythmic rise and fall
Of Negro voices in a chorus, all
The depth and vast infinitude of sound:
The battle moan of tribes with poisoned quiver
Above the cadence of a jungle river,
The scourge of lashing waves like many whips
Upon the beaten shoulders of slave-ships,
The ebb and flow of sorrow and of wrong
Now breaking into freedom and to song.

Farona Konopak

LARGO

As shadows slipping along the wall, women
Shawled in black pass down the packed dirt road.
Short black pyramids, changeless as all time,
They take themselves forever down the road.
So silently, so slowly, do they move,
From afar they are but shadows lingering
A sun-space on the low adobe wall.

Alfred Kreymborg

UNDER GLASS

If I could catch that moth,
that fluttering wayward thing
which beats about inside me all the day and half the night
(an insignificant net could certainly do it),
I'd stick him through the head
with a pin that's long and thin,
a pin that's long and strong enough to mount him under glass
(an insignificant pin could certainly do it);
I'd discover once for all
the color of his wings,
the nature of those crazy things that fooled me all these years:
purple, red or blue,
yellow, white or black,
or whether they're one and all of these and a shade or two besides
(an insignificant harmony or dissonance they could be);
I'd learn them once for all,
I'd know them, every vein,
so clear to all my neighbors, so invisible to me!

CREDO

Do fishes gleam with hope or flowers feel
The need of living still another life?
Do drowsy snakes, when skins begin to peel,
Dream of a sky where there's an end to strife?
Which of the idols cause such heads to nod?
Whom do the insects ask for one more day?
Do all the toads that dread the coming sod
Hop with the hope their present lives will pay?
Or does Man kneel alone with his high fancies?
Why can't he rest awhile among his senses?

No sooner does the sun return, he dances
With a gold and silver round of future tenses.
He who can make the most of transient skies,
It seems to me deserves the only prize.

HUMAN THRONE

No matter where I turn my head
Or turn it where it has to turn,
My eye will see me through, he said,
And saw him through another self
Turning his way, though he was dead.

This other self was in the world
For him to find the mirror of,
And through the person of the earth,
Of men embodied in his love,
Rose in time to another birth.

And so where Homer had no sight
But vision gave the centuries
A Grecian and a grander life:
An Iliad to brave the night,
An Odyssey to cross the seas,

Thus it is with the soul today
That simply cannot shine alone,
But gives to the poor land everywhere
Breath for a more than mortal air,
Breadth for a common sky and throne.

Fania Kruger

WANDERING CHILD

Now in your hour of song
    There is no sun,
And night falls before
    Your day has begun.

Oh, that a groping child
    Should whisper grace
With hunger deeply drawn
Upon his face.

Alexander Laing

DAVID TODAY

*Written as of 18th August, 1940;
published 9th August, 1941*

Your blood runs muddled,
My polyglot,
From Dutch and English
And Welsh and Scot;
But to honor you
In this year of shame,
We have named you David,
A Jewish name.
Upon your hand—
A scant inch long—
We lay the sense
Of your brother's wrong.

To this frail case
Of gristle and skin
We trust the fortunes
Of all your kin—
Your Negro brother,
Your brother the Jew—
Of all who suffer
From being few.

In cruel times
For a child to share
Your mother has dropped you,
Well aware
That flesh must carry
The mind's high stake,
Since the world we have
Is the world we make.

Let nothing rob you
Of discontent.
Your thin, first protest
Was early spent—
A cradle tempest,
Not loud, not long—
But your puny anger
Will yet be strong;
And we bid you nurse it,
While we nurse you,
To turn on Gentiles
Who hate the Jew,
On gentlemen
Who in pride of race
Would burn black problems
They dare not face.

Poor and lucky,
We can ill afford
A silver spoon
Or a silver cord;

But your name is David—
We bring you, instead,
One smooth flat stone
From the clean brook bed,
And with this for birthright
May you, at length,
Have little of comfort,
Much of strength.
We could wish you homeless
Under a ledge
With a mind that burns
Through the skull's thin edge—
Better so,
In the sleety rain,
Than plump and cozy
In belly and brain.

For there's work to be done
And all's not well.
The giants we fostered
Are yours to fell.
The peace we squandered
Is yours to win,
By anger flashed outward
And hate held in.
Let these be single
When each is great:
Anger blown clear
Of the coals of hate—
Keep hate for ideas,
Anger for men,
Now the fools of evil
Are loose again.

And when metals cancel
And wits lock fast,
One smooth flat stone
Can win, at the last,

Through fear and the will
To master fear
With the sling of David.

The giants are here.

Gordon Lawrence

THIRD AVENUE

It isn't only where the tall wood ferns
scatter their rusty spores on moss-cool earth,
or where the pale eye of the brown owl burns
and the thin, hungry fungus threads give birth,
sudden, enormous, to the white mushrooms,
like giants conjured from enchanted tombs.

It isn't only where the faintest breeze
turns the dry leaf, the yellow leaf again,
where birds cry lonely from the roofs of trees,
and crows sit blackly in white winter rain,
and all of summer's green designs are furled
in the long brooding of the Northern world.

Beneath the elevated tracks today
as cold a light falls on an empty building,
crystal of long ago and far away,
the starved grey spider in her cobweb gilding,
falls on a window of abandoned stuff,
turns it to palest gold, untrapped, aloof.

MUSEUM PIECE

Lo, there were giants in old days
When thunderous creatures strode the earth,

And tall fantastics came to birth
In darkness, in equivocal ways.
Beneath green fronds of mottled trees,
Behemoth, grave, incurious, rambled,
And the horned apparitions shambled,
Grim, by the shores of grey seas.
Staring-eyed, unwieldy things
Climbed the clear air on naked wings
Past the moth phantoms drifting by
And the green-lacquered dragonfly.

The old fantastics prowl no more.
All their cold armor's buried deep,
And all their heritage is sleep,
And all their fame is pedants' lore.
Yet through steep canyons of the mind
The vast hulks trample down the years,
Like a doomed army bright with spears,
Stupendous, impotent, and blind.

Ruth Lechlitner

SONG OF STARLINGS

In a great elm against the winter sky
Today I watched a cloud of starlings swing
Like dark leaves from the leafless boughs. And high
Blown by the wind, I heard them whistling:
Soft in the sharp light there I heard them sing.

What chance vibrations sprung from accident
Or secret law, this moment interlace
Song from a bird's throat, and the ear's intent
Bone listening, this bright earth tipped in space,
Birth, war, and death, and snow upon my face?

No one shall guess from what supremest need
These threads were knit; from what immensity
Mated with time, came forth the smallest seed
That life might flower, and that there might be
The cry of starlings from a leafless tree.

ONLY THE YEARS

Sea shell and flower corolla and strict blade of a wing,
The thigh's clean line, the pure curve of the breast—
All natural objects bred to the final form, the simple thing
Out of time past,

These flawless know survival. Year upon long year served
Their special use, shaping design to need:
The shell's enameled cone, the tapering thigh, the carved
And segment-fitted seed.

Down through the generations craftsmen, creators
Have passed the gift of power from palm to palm—
Gift dreamed in the laboring mind, taken in love greatly,
Alive and warm,

Nor ripped in one stroke from the body, bloodless and shining,
Nor hacked out raw from the secreting stone
Came the essential thing, the ultimate simple line
Exact, alone.

(How many ages blind, till the seeking eye might prove
In light through glass one cell's minute perfection,
—Years motion-locked till the piston functioned smooth
As the heel's tendon?)

Men of our time, workers in wood, fabric or metal
Strip ornament from structure: beauty is line
In use: the bridge harp-cabled, the ship's deep keel
The wing-spread of the plane.

But not in our time, not yet, is the pattern for life drawn clean:
The mind's unserved, the flesh misused, the breath

Chokes in the terrible net spread dark between
Our birth and death.

When shall we strip off the false and intricate decay
That rival nations value: in what hour
Strike the tools of craft from the hands of madness, save
The gift of power?

Only the years that lie on the far edge of light
Shall answer us, the possible future see
Tempered in blood and fire beyond this shadow of our night
The simple form set free.

Richard LeGallienne

WHAT OF THE DARKNESS?
(To the Happy Dead People)

What of the darkness? Is it very fair?
Are there great calms? and find we silence there?
Like soft-shut lilies, all your faces glow
With some strange peace our faces never know,
With some great faith our faces never dare,—
Dwells it in Darkness? Do you find it there?

Is it a Bosom where tired heads may lie?
Is it a Mouth to kiss our weeping dry?
Is it a Hand to still the pulse's leap?
Is it a Voice that holds the runes of sleep?
Day shows us not such comfort anywhere—
Dwells it in Darkness? Do you find it there?

Out of the Day's deceiving light we call—
Day that shows man so great and God so small,

That hides the stars and magnifies the grass—
O is the Darkness too a lying glass!
Or, undistracted, do you find truth there?
What of the Darkness? Is it very fair?

Laura Lourene LeGear

WATER MOCCASIN

Eve, with her warm lips redder
Than skin of reddening apple,
Pleases the fern-green adder,
Wearing the shadow's dapple;

Artless Eve, earth's first blossom,
Shaming the lilies' stipple,
Wakened beside the balsam,
Watches the catkins topple;

Eve, slender as her serpent
Coiled near a yellow aster,
Her sleep as cool and sentient,
Beds in the mallow cluster.

In Eden still, long after,
I lie among wild mosses,
And answer with light laughter,
The scaly one who passes!

Mary Sinton Leitch

HE WHO LOVES THE OCEAN

He who loves the ocean
And the ways of ships
May taste beside a mountain pool
Brine on his lips:

May feel in the desert
The parched day long
The slow camels swaying
To the sea's song.

A meadow in the moonlight,
However dry it be,
Is slippery with seaweed,
Smells of the sea.

He who is banished
From marshes and weirs,
Who has for sea savor
The salt of his tears,

To him the dust of hoofbeats
On a windless plain
Shall be spindrift flying
Before the hurricane.

In cornfield or wheatfield,
Wherever he may go,
He hears water sobbing
Low . . . low . . .

He hears water calling
Till a prairie mist is thinned
To skysails and royals
Proud in the wind.

Whom the sea has summoned,
Whom ocean claims her own,
He finds in clouds a caravel
And coral in a stone:

He looks toward lost horizons
Till any city street
May dance and dip and curvet
Under his feet.

Who lives a salt sea lover,
Though inland far he dies,
Feels sea wind on his pillow,
Has the North Star in his eyes.

Jessie Lemont

DIANA REMEMBERS ACTAEON

You came once through the blue dusk of the evening,
Your yellow hair the color of the sun's gold,
Blown backward like a bird's wings from your forehead
Brushed by the wind's breath;

Beneath dark brows, straight as a tense-strung bowstring,
Your grey eyes flashed the lightnings of the summer—
Your smile mysteriously gleaming as the moonlight,
Your mouth a crescent.

Your ears laid tight against your head, sloped backward,
Like those of creatures of the forest fastness
That listen in the silence to earth's secrets,
You moved with fleetness—

Your throat's proud column lifted from strong shoulders,
Your supple flanks sloped down to delicate ankles,

Your long step made no sound through the green arches
As you came toward me—

Your eyes on mine—as star-fire drowns in nightpools—
And every leaf was hushed upon the branches.
Time stopped—Nothing stirred in the deepening darkness——
And then—the hounds leapt! . . .

William Ellery Leonard

SONNETS FROM "TWO LIVES"

Death hath two hands to slay with: with the one
He stabs the loveliness of Yesterday,
Till all its gold and blue is sodden gray
To memory forever, in the sun:
Think ye I think upon our earliest kiss,
Our walks, our vines, our readings, as I would
Were she still by me in her womanhood
To join in tender talk on all of this?
Death hath two hands to slay with: with the other
He stabs the glory of our bright Tomorrow—
Our best reality, our younger brother,
Our spirit-self—upon the fields of sorrow:
Think ye he took no unbuilt house from me,
No unsailed voyage with her across the sea?

Thrice summer and autumn passed into the west,
Across her grave with flower and leaf they passed,
Thrice winter with his moon. Now spring at last—
The fatal spring of her supreme unrest
And ultimate hour—its green young feet hath pressed
Once more on hills and fields and brought to us
From southern oceans small birds amorous
To build in trees of song the happy nest

Above her grave . . . And meanwhile in the world
Fire, flood, and whirlwind smote the planted ground,
And ships with lights and music sank at sea,
And flags o'er new-born nations were unfurled,
And men discovered, as the earth went round,
New stars off yonder in eternity.

May Lewis

DAYS AT SEA

This level ocean, flat and circular
As a thin disk of steel, a widespread wheel,
Holds at its centre, day after passing day,
The driving ship that seemingly pursues
From one unchanging spot its outward way.

Horizon-locked, the speeding engines make
No headway toward the single curving line
That lies so sharp, so dangerously fine
Against the sky, it might, indeed, cut through—
Like some huge circular saw, nick a quick gash,
Inflict a cosmic flaw
Where we, ship-prisoned, would espy the flash
Of a new zodiac's forbidden sign.

Thus the mind idles while the eye must pace,
Hunger-compelled, the compass points of space
Seeking its natural food: shape, form—birds, trees,
Or failing these, at least the raised irregular waves of storm.
But the ring holds, in cold persistency, nothing
But empty sky, unyielding sea.
O ship, strive forward, speed!—let engines roar;
Force from the circle a straight line of shore.

THE GRASS

How is the grass set free?
What liberates the green?
Is there some urging need,
Some inkling of that upper, far-spread scene,
Wedged in the seed,
That wills: go forth and be?

How can the tiny grains
Held under heavy earth,
In that moist, smothering crown
Foresee the sunlight's worth,
Or dare, when that hard surface holds them down,
To suffer thrusting pains?

Is it from earth's deep heart,
That edict: Unhusk; go!
You shall behold a sky . . .
Undoubtedly, blades know
A motion to leap high,
Something that makes them start.

Or, from an ambient sun,
Perhaps, through miles of air
There falls a foreign word
Descriptive of how fair
To see the thunderous rain—the singing bird—
The white snow lightly spun!

Now the brave answer spreads—
Even the rock is glad;
The green—the green is here!
The naked suffering of the earth is clad;
A velvet folds the sphere;
The cattle bend their heads.

Elias Lieberman

TO MY BROTHERS EVERYWHERE

Test me not for shibboleth;
   Like a king, anointed, ermined,
I was born into a faith
   And my skin was predetermined.

Bearing burdens on my back
   You will find me everywhere;
Tropic suns have turned me black,
   Northern winds have bleached me fair.

But the heart within me beats
   Just like yours in utter blindness
To the rhythm of the streets
   To an act of hate or kindness.

Though my house be paradise,
   Every wall is made of glass;
May the question in my eyes
   Brush your spirit as I pass.

By the sacrament of pain
   Men must share with one another,
By the hopes we nursed in vain
You will know me, O my brother.

SITTING-ROOM IN A BOWERY HOTEL
(Nocturne)

Pain is a rat that gnaws away the heart;
   It nibbles nerves and leaves a vacuum,
Until the breast no longer feels a dart,
   Until the ear no longer hears a drum.
And so the forms that slump in wooden chairs
   Are proof against the stirring things they read
By feeble light; if taken unawares,
   They look like shapes whose souls have gone to seed.

Each rustling paper is an anodyne
  Against the hours whose curse it is to drag.
These men are in retreat, a broken line;
  Their shell-torn citadels display no flag.
Grotesques are stumbling over graves to keep
A rendezvous with nothingness and sleep.

Anne Morrow Lindbergh

ELEGY UNDER THE STARS

I here; you there—
But under those eyes, space is all-where.

I alive; you dead—
But under those eyes, all-time is spread.

I alone—
But under those eyes, all things are joined;

All sorrow, and all beauty, and all spirit,
Are one.

Vachel Lindsay

ABRAHAM LINCOLN WALKS AT MIDNIGHT
In Springfield, Illinois

It is portentous, and a thing of state
That here at midnight in our little town,
A mourning figure walks, and will not rest,
Near the old court-house pacing up and down.

Or by his homestead, or in shadowed yards,
He lingers where his children used to play;
Or through the market, on the well-worn stones,
He stalks until the dawn-stars burn away.

A bronzed lank man! His suit of ancient black,
A famous high top-hat and plain worn shawl,
Make him the quaint great figure that men love,
The prairie lawyer, master of us all.

He cannot sleep upon his hillside now.
He is among us—as in times before!
And we who toss and lie awake for long
Breathe deep, and start, to see him pass the door.

His head is bowed. He thinks on men and kings.
Yea, when the sick world cries, how can he sleep?
Too many peasants fight, they know not why;
Too many homesteads in black terror weep.

The sins of all the war-lords burn his heart.
He sees the dreadnaughts scouring every main.
He carries on his shawl-wrapped shoulders now
The bitterness, the folly and the pain.

He cannot rest until a spirit-dawn
Shall come—the shining hope of Europe free:
The league of sober folk, the Workers' Earth,
Bringing long peace to Cornland, Alp and Sea.

It breaks his heart that kings must murder still,
That all his hours of travail here for men
Seem yet in vain. And who will bring white peace
That he may sleep upon his hill again?

Carolyn Wilson Link

APOLOGY TO MY HEIRS

My mother's father's father from his field
Gathered the stone because the stone was there,
To build the house that was the land's first yield;
Felled his own timber to shape sill and stair.
Deep-walled against the heat and cold it grew,
The solid stone elastic to his need;
When he was gone, he would be host, he knew,
To generations of his spreading seed.
Defeating time itself, his home will stand,
Though aliens mend the roof and till the land.
    There was time then to live.

My father's father, when the trees were small,
Set cedars out where his forefathers lay,
Now merged in this rough-textured living wall;
His mother, kneeling on a sunny day,
Tamped roots of lily-of-the-valley in,
That since have knit a thick and glossy cover.
Cedars are not more upright than such men,
Nor lilies sweet as those they blossom over.
Centuries later, under simple stones,
The curious spade will crunch on honest bones.
    There was time then to die.

To you, my heirs, who even as you turn
The radio low, impatient of my warning,
Protest that empires fall, and you must learn
Which will survive, for History in the morning;
Who, in beginning, face fantastic ends,
Pitifully armed with words upon a page,
I penitently make no more amends
Than to remind you of your heritage.
The world is wilderness again; to you
The challenge falls. Oh, tame it, make it new!
    There is still time.

Gordden Link

THE DEAF

Out of the darkness, out of the years, out of the
    mind's reluctant hoardings,
faintly the whisper reaches, then recedes, faintly
    the sound describes a circle
far out of reach. Caught on the perilous edge
    of vague concentric impulse,
the ears, spread tight against the precipice of
    hearing, precariously pluck a tremor
that seems to be more memory than sound. Here is
    adventure set to music
yet unheard, or heard too many seasons past; here
    is a wall
that needs quick climbing, or that was climbed too
    long ago. Or maybe it is no wall
at all. Perhaps this looming obstacle to understanding
    is sound unfiltered;
perhaps a strained attention yet will capture the fine
    elusive fugitive

of sound that hovers out of reach. We clench the hand,
    we bulge the jaw,
we wince and arch, yet bring the trembling wings of
    distant, or imagined, noise
no nearer, no slightest line's width nearer.

Out of the darkness, out of the years, out of the
    mind's reluctant hoardings,
comes what the braver know is memory; comes what the
    craven try to think
is tangible and present and recorded against the
    futile tightened drums
that hold their thinkings taut. Out of the darkness, out
    of the years, out of the mind's
invincible and fearless voyagings, the braver find
    a quiet peace,
a peace that mountains have, or seas, or clouds, to
    find themselves against a sky
that they may never touch. The braver go, happy in
    sight of birds
that fly with silent whirr, or brooks that have a
    silent splash, or boys that play
wildly in loud quiet. Out of the darkness, out of
    the years, out of the silent
orchestration minds can make, the braver march to
    a silent air,
lifting their eyes to the curious banners that crackle
    in silence, and watching their pennons
furled proud then whipped aloft by a silent wind.

Sarah Litsey

SKUNK CABBAGE RISING IN MARCH

Push up, push up! Your perilous tip
Is axis for this wind-torn day.
The slow unsealing of your lip
Speaks no soft syllable for May,

Tenders no fragile, April word.
Here in the bare and bloodless cold
The stern, omniscient voice is heard
Strike utterance from you, fold on fold.

And wind that shreds this ragged sky
Disturbes no segment of your plan.
Green at your heart the centuries lie
Unmindful of the hates of man.

Cleaving black water, bitter born,
Thrust wisdom ancient and unbroken
Into this day, wind-churned and torn
For lack of logic coldly spoken.

Anne Lloyd

TWO POWERS

There are two potent separate powers
That yet are one—
The urge of green that through dark hours,
Strives toward the sun;

And the descending fires that greet
The thrusting blade—
When these eternal lovers meet,
Harvests are made.

Amy Lowell

LILACS

Lilacs,
False blue,
White,
Purple
Color of lilac,
Your great puffs of flowers
Are everywhere in this my New England.
Among your heart-shaped leaves
Orange orioles hop like music-box birds and
    sing
Their little weak soft songs;
In the crooks of your branches
The bright eyes of song sparrows sitting on
    spotted eggs
Peer restlessly through the light and shadow
Of all Springs.
Lilacs in dooryards
Holding quiet conversations with an early moon;
Lilacs watching a deserted house
Settling sideways into the grass of an old road;
Lilacs, wind-beaten, staggering under a lop-sided
    shock of bloom
Above a cellar dug into a hill.
You are everywhere.

You were everywhere.
You tapped the window when the preacher preached
    his sermon,
And ran along the road beside the boy going to
    school.
You stood by pasture-bars to give the cows
    good milking,
You persuaded the housewife that her dish-pan was
    of silver
And her husband an image of pure gold.
You flaunted the fragrance of your blossoms
Through the wide doors of Custom Houses—
You, and sandalwood, and tea,
Charging the noses of quill-driving clerks
When a ship was in from China.
You called to them: "Goose-quill men, goose-
    quill men,
May is a month for flitting,"
Until they writhed on their high stools
And wrote poetry on their letter-sheets behind
    the propped-up ledgers.
Paradoxical New England clerks,
Writing inventories in ledgers, reading the
    "Song of Solomon" at night,
So many verses before bedtime,
Because it was the Bible.
The dead fed you
Amid the slant stones of graveyards.
Pale ghosts who planted you
Came in the night time
And let their thin hair blow through your
    · clustered stems.
You are of the green sea,
And of the stone hills which reach a long
    distance.
You are of elm-shaded streets with little shops
    where they sell kites and marbles,

You are of great parks where everyone walks and
    nobody is at home.
You cover the blind sides of greenhouses
And lean over the top to say a hurry-word through
    the glass
To your friends, the grapes, inside.

Lilacs,
False blue,
White,
Purple,
Color of lilac,
You have forgotten your Eastern origin,
The veiled women with eyes like panthers,
The swollen, aggressive turbans of jeweled Pashas.
Now you are a very decent flower,
A reticent flower,
A curiously clear-cut, candid flower,
Standing beside clean doorways,
Friendly to a house-cat and a pair of spectacles,
Making poetry out of a bit of moonlight
And a hundred or two sharp blossoms.

Maine knows you,
Has for years and years;
New Hampshire knows you,
And Massachusetts
And Vermont.
Cape Cod starts you along the beaches to Rhode Island;
Connecticut takes you from a river to the sea.
You are brighter than apples,
Sweeter than tulips,
You are the great flood of our souls
Bursting above the leaf-shapes of our hearts,
You are the smell of all Summers,
The love of wives and children,
The recollection of the gardens of little children,
You are State Houses and Charters

And the familiar treading of a foot to and fro on
    a road it knows.
May is lilac here in New England,
May is a thrush singing "Sun up!" on a tip-top
    ash-tree,
May is white clouds behind pine-trees
Puffed out and marching upon a blue sky.
May is a green as no other,
May is much sun through small leaves,
May is soft earth,
And apple-blossoms,
And windows open to a South wind.
May is a full light wind of lilac
From Canada to Narragansett Bay.

Lilacs,
False blue,
White,
Purple,
Color of lilac,
Heart-leaves of lilac all over New England,
Roots of lilac under all the soil of New England,
Liac in me because I am New England,
Because my roots are in it,
Because my leaves are of it,
Because my flowers are for it,
Because it is my country
And I speak to it of itself
And sing of it with my own voice
Since certainly it is mine.

Holger Lundbergh

WHEN A GULL FALLS

When a gull falls
The whole air calls,
The whole air sings
In pain and despair
As the shot rings
Out, and a wild flutter of wings
Shakes the air.
There is nothing quite so thoroughly dead
As a gull with the small hot lead
Hidden under white feathers turning red.
No more utterly difficult sight
Than the wide symmetry of a gull's flight
Shattered and wasted in a drunken downward plunge,
A wheeling, tumbling lunge,
And a swift, splashy fall.
And there is nothing, quite nothing at all,
Like the sudden surprise and fright,
The horrible, futile shame,
That burns like a flame,
Fiercely hot as the sun,
In the heart of the man with the gun.

Gertrude May Lutz

GOLGOTHA

This was the cross then, O not this solid weight
yoked over shoulder bone
        bruising the flesh;
not this long length of wood,
not the dust furrowing,
        tears and the thorned blood
        smeared where the feet had walked.
This was the cross
stretched on the face of men:
men, sprung with tiger mouths:
        snarl of a tiger;
men, sharp of fang and claw,
        wild of eye-glitter.
Up to Golgotha: O wear the cross
dark behind eyelids
                and the mind seared with it.

CONCEPT

        See: in the pallid distances, the star,
Its light a shallowness against a shuttered earth;
And the shepherds standing in the bloody meadows
Lean their blindness upon a bladeless sword,
        Bringing their minds back to beginnings:
O, know this emptiness!
                Look now: divide the years:
This field is midnight lost with sheep, and camel
Caravans line the east and no shape of them:
Even their bells sounding with brittle silences.

O, where are the wise men,
                The moon-round saddle bags?

Maureen Cobb Mabbott

IMPERIOUS DESIGN

The branch of plum
Escaped the vase,
The hand's intent,
The full, white phrase

Described design
Imperiously,
To nothing bent
Except the tree;

How like the mind
Revealed its root,
Spoke bloom and meant
The red plum fruit.

Christy MacKaye

SPEECH

The wind storms down the desert with more speed,
Over smooth rock, and over voiceless plain—
With greater speech—more many-hued with pain—
Than ever she has sung through growing reed,
Or peopled forest, or dry shard of seed:
And so in desert stillness let my brain
Be empty in pure waiting, and restrain
All piping of its sharp, up-starting weed.

Level my words as smooth as sea-worn shell;
Let no crag tune the wind, no mica turn
The sky's light to itself with glistening;
But through them clearly let the broad winds tell
Talk of the stars to stone—what raindrops learn
While lying in the sunlight, listening.

Percy MacKaye

MY LOVE AND I
(To Marion Morse MacKaye)

1896

My love was freshly come from sea
The morning she first greeted me:
The salt mist's tang, the sunny blow
Had tinged her cheeks a ripening glow.

She bowed to me with all the ease
Of meadow-grasses in the breeze,
And yet her look seemed far away
Amid the splendors of the spray.

Her step was vigorous and free
As maiden's in the Odyssey;
And when she laughed, I heard the tunes
Of rushes in the windy dunes.

An air so limitless, an eye
So virgin in its royalty—
Hers was a spirit and a form
That took my inland heart by storm.

I felt an impulse, an unrest,
And secret tides within my breast
Flowed up, with silent, glad control,
And drew the rivers of my soul.

1939

My love and I went wandering
 Deep in sweet woods together.
The spring of her step made all the paths
 Of May-time bloom in her weather,
And the way she went, wherever she turned
 Joy followed in her tether.

  O, tune, tune,
  Tune of her springing
  Step, in your swinging,
How blithe you sprung toward the eve of June!

My love and I went wondering
 Up in great boughs and under.
The breath of her heart made all the birds
 To tune their own to her wonder,
Till the break of my heart in the darkening wood
 Rent all our boughs asunder.

  O, tune, tune,
  Tune of her breathing
  Heart, in your wreathing—
Why did you die in the dawn of June?

Sister M. Madeleva

NOVEMBER AFTERNOONS

Now they have come, these afternoons in November,
When all the air is still and branches are bare,
And the long, lovely light that I remember
Invades with luminous peace the untroubled air.

Off to the west a dozen trees together
Stand in gray loveliness, bemused with light;
Slender and silver they stand in the autumn weather,
Waiting the inevitable winter, the inevitable night.

Blossoming light they bear as a single flower,
And silence more singing sweet than a lone bird's call.
Off to the west I stand, sharing their hour,
At peace with beauty and needing no song at all.

RIDDLES, ONE, TWO, AND THREE

My lover is a fool more wise
Than Solomon;
My lover is a bird that flies
Into the Sun.

He is a lighted lamp, my love,
A midnight cry,
A mortal worm that died to prove
He could not die.

My lover is a cedar tree
With branches spread;
A sweet and bitter fruit is he,
Alive and dead.

My lover is a quiet rain
Falling on fleece;

My lover is or endless pain
Or endless peace

Or sometime an instinctive mole
Breaking the clod;
My lover is a thief who stole
The name of God.

Edwin Markham

LINCOLN, THE MAN OF THE PEOPLE

When the Norn Mother saw the Whirlwind Hour
Greatening and darkening as it hurried on,
She left the Heaven of Heroes and came down
To make a man to meet the mortal need.
She took the tried clay of the common road—
Clay warm yet with the genial heat of Earth,
Dashed through it all a strain of prophecy;
Tempered the heap with thrill of human tears;
Then mixed a laughter with the serious stuff.
Into the shape she breathed a flame to light
That tender, tragic, ever-changing face.
Here was a man to hold against the world,
A man to match the mountains and the sea.

The color of the ground was in him, the red earth;
The smack and tang of elemental things;
The rectitude and patience of the cliff;
The good-will of the rain that loves all leaves;
The friendly welcome of the wayside well;
The courage of the bird that dares the sea;
The gladness of the wind that shakes the corn;
The pity of the snow that hides all scars;

The secrecy of streams that make their way
Beneath the mountain to the rifted rock;
The tolerance and equity of light
That gives as freely to the shrinking flower
As to the great oak flaring to the wind—
To the grave's low hill as to the Matterhorn
That shoulders out the sky.

                           Sprung from the West,
The strength of virgin forests braced his mind,
The hush of spacious prairies stilled his soul.
Up from log cabin to the Capitol,
One fire was on his spirit, one resolve—
To send the keen ax to the root of wrong,
Clearing a free way for the feet of God.
And evermore he burned to do his deed
With the fine stroke and gesture of a king:
He built the rail-pile as he built the State,
Pouring his splendid strength through every blow,
The conscience of him testing every stroke,
To make his deed the measure of a man.

So came the Captain with the mighty heart;
And when the judgment thunders split the house,
Wrenching the rafters from their ancient rest,
He held the ridgepole up, and spiked again
The rafters of the Home. He held his place—
Held the long purpose like a growing tree—
Held on through blame and faltered not at praise.
And when he fell in whirlwind, he went down
As when a lordly cedar, green with boughs,
Goes down with a great shout upon the hills,
And leaves a lonesome place against the sky.

Lenore G. Marshall

THIS TWENTIETH CENTURY MIND

This twentieth century mind
Betrayed by its own reason
Trusting in no known light
Stands in an open prison.

It has the skeptic fact
Tethered, explored, and sure,
Amended, ever intact;
It has an old desire.

Its pierced secret belief
Flowing on like a dark river,
Long ages harbored and safe,
Still seeks its own, forever.

So honeycombed by faith
But without faith in its vision
It would pray, if there were prayer,
Too wise for the heart's decision.

Asks nothing and all of fate,
Outwits itself securely:
We have found our love too late,
We have lost our love too early.

AS THOUGH FROM LOVE
(Proust, in his last book)

Out of the matrix
Of those lies
Light pierced as though
They had been verities.

At last O at last
Darkness grew so blind
That the heart broke;
Found egress through the mind.

Then from barren room
And bleak door
Creeping from bitter place
Sorrows turned servitor

Against whom contending
New vistas rose
As though from love, as though from hope,
                    as though
They had been verities.

The shadowy past
Stands like a bed
Where matings were,
From whence this seed was bred

Whose roots plunge deeply
Into grief;
Old memories
Inhabit stones with life

And make strange faces
Sudden kin,
Recovering time:
No longer now alone.

What bent key opened up
The dust?
What world retrieved
From a world lost?

The various hours
Vainly spent
Became a glass,
An instrument

Wherein to discern
What had been blank before,
The lineaments of night.
Sorrows turned servitor,

Against whom contending
Through all those lies,
Light, immaculate, pierced as though
They had been verities.

Gilbert Maxwell

"IT WAS GOOD FOR THE HEBREW CHILDREN . . ."

Whether at noon or dawn this ship was steered
into the blameless seas . . .
whether southeast or north her compass veered,
yet was her course due west; and not for these
uncomprehending, but for a hopeful world,
her time of sailing midnight in the mind.
Not for these soft-eyed exiles at the rail
watching the water where the sun strikes blind
the eye with sheaths of silver . . . not for them
such knowledge as we have of fang and scale
and tentacled, hidden terror . . . slim and pale
and each alone they stand, complacent Shem
and Ham and Japheth . . . eagerly they stare
starboard and port, not knowing as we know
the prow of no ship now points anywhere
toward any land where it is safe to go.

David McCord

A STAR BY DAY

A star that burst one afternoon
Between me and the earth-lit moon,
And saved some field from being plowed,
Became, as once it was, a cloud.

Some vagrancy had made me pause
For heaven to punctuate a clause,
To drop her comma in the blue,
Though legible to very few.

Better, perhaps: a star that spoke
In simple terms of fire and smoke,
But soundless with the stale report
Of ancient wars and dragon snort.

I saw it flare and turn to fleece
And in the air obtain release:
A cloud for those who looked too late
To see what meteors create.

I leaned against some solid stone
Or brick that I could call my own
And, fearful of the universe,
I watched another world disperse.

It feathered out, the way of mist
And not of iron-spark and grist:
You couldn't tell for losing shape
It wasn't what it set to ape.

Perhaps some fragment came to grief
As, with a lesser turn, the leaf;
And let the upper current lift
Its greater part in subtle rift.

But most, I thought, it wasn't strange
That stars will shoot beyond their range,
Beyond their time and normal spread,
And fall to earth in daylight, dead.

We've built so much against the dark
In brilliant room and flooded park,
And come so far beyond the night
A star by day is only right.

Virginia Taylor McCormick

APOSTROPHE TO A FIGHTER PLANE

I saw you rise into the sun, trim-lined,
Your coat of grey, tri-colour decoration,
Higher and higher on your way to find
New routes to east or west, the swift mutation
From earth-born mechanism to silver bird;
Cutting the air with wings no bird has known
To sound of music only the spheres have heard
At heights to which no feathered thing has flown.

Yet, greater than you, more beautiful and brave
The lad who charts your course, nerves tense as wire,
His brain attuned to every aerial wave,
His heart aflame with Galahad's old fire.
Oh silver bird, forget not that you bear
Some mother's son through those vast fields of air.

Alice Monks Mears

BRIEF ENTERPRISE

Others knew the lazily-shepherded summer years,
the sunny, irised ledges of the onetime years,
the sense of time only like a noon-still light
hearted with a far bell; knew all that is ancient as the lute,
idyllic, silent, forgotten. They held in hand the half-grown
feather-breasted hours, wing-clipped against flight,
stroked to song; put the teeth to some warm dripping fruit
as they lay in the slow soundless shadow cooling the stone.

Envy them if you will, but this plummeting time,
the whir of these metallic years, this time
of splintered night, violent day, must strike the mind awake.
Vision of races: how we millions and millions plunge and pour
through strange skies, meteorites and fragments of
what inconstant star! must finally shake
and exhaust the little ego—clean it to the steely core
which is indivisible man and his brief enterprise of love.

WHAT SPIRIT?

What spirit do I house?
It drinks no ease of night,
the starred wine-bowl. It wakes
restless still when the dawn-wave breaks
in crested gold-flaked light
around the anchored mountains' prows.

What was its other name,
what its surmise of death,
that (unbidden by the mind)
night and day it must search to find
beyond "the Lord God saith"
some knowledge hid in flint and flame?

It flees the hungry sense
which color, texture, sound
can fill and fill again.
Shall spirit need no beauty then,
feeling a hunger more profound,
glimpsing fulfillment more intense?

I do not know its need.
I know it does not rest.
Yet once it paused, nor stirred,
listening to love—as though it heard
half-answer to its earth-doomed quest
within the silence of the seed.

Marjorie Meeker

THE MAGNOLIA TREE

It is not that the magnolia tree is not beautiful
          and strange
     With the phallus-like buds and the moon-white
          blossoms showing
Pale through dark leaves, and the mocking bird
          singing with the change
     Of the land's to the sea-wind's blowing.

But that there you walked, in your hands the head-
          lines accursed
     Staring up through the leafy shadows; and the
          words you said
Will ring down far years. Yes, I know. But you
          said them first
     Walking in that green shade.

Now the year's at full circle. It is spring. It
    is deep bright May
And the great white flowers are unfolding once
    more. I know their scent.
But I have not seen the bloom. I do not go that way
    Nor any way you went.

It is not that the magnolia tree is not beautiful
    and rare
    But that my mind asks: Where are you? What
    of the strict swift words
Silenced, and through green branches no voice there
    But the false sweet mocking bird's.

Gerard Previn Meyer

THERE IS A STREET

There is a street in town I know
where all the houses in the row
are echo echo of each other:
brick and brick are sister, brother,
life and death are just the same
and nobody has a different name,
nobody even has a number
or other property to cumber
with separate identity:
even the seasons there agree,
spring with winter,
summer with fall,
the self-same minter
molds them all.

The day begins at half-past equal
and every day has the self-same sequel.

Nobody says a different word
and everybody is interred
with the very thought
that a person ought
to have in a street
where everyone's feet
walk with a rhythm never broken
just as if God had never spoken.

Edna St. Vincent Millay

ON HEARING A SYMPHONY OF BEETHOVEN

Sweet sounds. Oh, beautiful music, do not cease!
Reject me not into the world again.
With you alone is excellence and peace,
Mankind made plausible, his purpose plain.
Enchanted in your air benign and shrewd,
With limbs a-sprawl and empty faces pale,
The spiteful and the stingy and the rude
Sleep like the scullions in the fairy-tale.
This moment is the best the world can give:
The tranquil blossom on the tortured stem.
Reject me not, sweet sounds! oh, let me live,
Till Doom espy my towers and scatter them,
A city spell-bound under the aging sun,
Music my rampart, and my only one.

TO JESUS ON HIS BIRTHDAY

For this your mother sweated in the cold,
For this you bled upon the bitter tree:
A yard of tinsel ribbon bought and sold;

A paper wreath; a day at home for me.
The merry bells ring out, the people kneel;
Up goes the man of God before the crowd;
With voice of honey and with eyes of steel
He drones your humble gospel to the proud.
Nobody listens. Less than the wind that blows
Are all your words to us you died to save.
O Prince of Peace! O Sharon's dewy Rose!
How mute you lie within your vaulted grave.
    The stone the angel rolled away with tears
    Is back upon your mouth these thousand years.

THE BUCK IN THE SNOW

White sky, over the hemlocks bowed with snow,
Saw you not at the beginning of evening the antlered
    buck and his doe
Standing in the apple-orchard? I saw them. I saw them
    suddenly go,
Tails up, with long leaps lovely and slow,
Over the stone-wall into the wood of hemlocks
    bowed with snow.

Now lies he here, his wild blood scalding the snow.

How strange a thing is death, bringing to his knees,
    bringing to his antlers
The buck in the snow.
How strange a thing,—a mile away by now, it may be,
Under the heavy hemlocks that as the moments pass
Shift their loads a little, letting fall a feather
    of snow—
Life, looking out attentive from the eyes of the doe.

Joaquin Miller

COLUMBUS
(August 3–October 12, 1492)

Behind him lay the gray Azores,
 Behind the Gates of Hercules;
Before him not the ghost of shores,
 Before him only shoreless seas.

The good mate said: "Now must we pray,
 For lo! the very stars are gone.
Brave Admiral, speak, what shall I say?"
 "Why, say 'Sail on! sail on! and on!' "

"My men grow mutinous day by day;
 My men grow ghastly wan and weak."
The stout mate thought of home; a spray
 Of salt wave washed his swarthy cheek.
"What shall I say, brave Admiral, say,
 If we sight naught but seas at dawn?"
"Why, you shall say at break of day,
 'Sail on! sail on! sail on! and on!' "

They sailed and sailed, as winds might blow,
 Until at last the blanched mate said:
"Why, now not even God would know
 Should I and all my men fall dead.
These very winds forget their way,
 For God from these dread seas is gone.
Now speak, brave Admiral, speak and say"—
 He said: "Sail on! sail on! and on!"

They sailed. They sailed. Then spake the mate:
 "This mad sea shows his teeth to-night.
He curls his lip, he lies in wait,
 With lifted teeth, as if to bite!

Brave Admiral, say but one good word:
    "What shall we do when hope is gone?"
The words leapt like a leaping sword:
    "Sail on! sail on! sail on! sail on!"

Then, pale and worn, he kept his deck,
    And peered through darkness. Ah, that night
Of all dark nights! And then a speck—
    A light! a light! a light! a light!
It grew, a starlit flag unfurled!
    It grew to be Time's burst of dawn.
He gained a world; he gave that world
    Its grandest lesson: "On! sail on!"

Mary Owings Miller

CAMOUFLAGE OF THE WILLOW PTARMIGAN

Covert and quill lie thick and white as floes
In Yukon dusks.
Limb-shadows which band his back are bare as rows
Of ivory tusks.

He clings on the ice with creepers, talon-sharp.
His sight is keen
As wind which hums with deep tones of a harp.
He is not seen

By searching fox nor circling bird of prey
So white, so still
Do carven feathers lie. No signs betray
The warning thrill

Set up by crimson coursing through his veins,
By tensing claws—
As past his ears with the doom of hurricanes
Move swift fox-paws.

Virginia Scott Miner

MOUSE IN A FLORIST'S WINDOW

Behold this Easter guest who goes
From sculptored lily to frail rose;
O see how small, how fleetly dun
This tremble-tailed and swiftfoot one.

But why he came, with what vast plans in mind,
We shall not know—and yet perhaps shall find
The thought of him like tiny Life-in-Death,
Absurdity and beauty, in a breath!

Edith Mirick

DROUGHT

The spring that welled once from this meadow-hill
Is dry now, and the moss that comforted
The edge is gone. Strike the rock if you will,
But no stream bubbles forth. Something is dead
In the hill's heart that rippled out in sweet
Clear crystal for the bird, that could assuage

A summer's fever, wet the slender feet
Of the curled fern in a green hermitage.

Dry is the hollow where we stooped to drink,
Dry as the spring of grief which grows too great
For word or tear, leaving the stubbled brink
Of old despair—lips inarticulate,
With no more visible sign, nor whispered sound
Than wells here from the seamed and barren ground.

Harriet Monroe

THE WATER OUZEL

Little brown surf-bather of the mountains!
Spirit of foam, lover of cataracts, shaking your wings
    in falling waters!
Have you no fear of the roar and rush
    when Nevada plunges—
Nevada, the shapely dancer, feeling her way with
    slim white fingers?
How dare you dash at Yosemite the mighty—
Tall, white-limbed Yosemite, leaping down, down,
    over the cliff?
Is it not enough to lean on the blue air of mountains?
Is it not enough to rest with your mate at timber-line
    in bushes that hug the rocks?
Must you fly through mad waters
    where the heaped-up granite breaks them?
Must you batter your wings in the torrent?
Must you plunge for life or death through the foam?

Vaida Stewart Montgomery

I AM DESERT-BORN

The cactus has its spike,
    The prickly-pear its spears;
I shall have the like
    All of my years.

For I am desert-born,
    Stinging those who pass,
As the mesquite thorn
    And the needle-grass.

I am desert-born,
    And the desert marks its young
With spike or spear or thorn
    Or a sharp tongue.

Edwin Morgan

AT THE SHORE

Before that ship, there was no motion,
Before that bird, there was no light:
Just the gray furrows of an ocean,
Just a sky turning into night.

And I had been as not before
In broad deep distances alone:
Just a cold rippling over stone
And the wind whitening the shore.

Yet the dark heart would not be still,
The body would not peaceful lie,
With hopes a sky could not fulfill,
And fear seas could not purify.

That gust of darkening mist was sweet,
The drear uneasy ocean's breath,
Where, whispering quietly of death,
The wistful ghosts of the deathless meet.

And that bleak unsubstantial sky
Blew dark upon a cloud of white,
And, feeling its empty coldness, I
Knew it would yield no more than night.

The night made one of sea and bird
And sky in a sharply still embrace;
And I turned in the dark for a hand or face
Or some inconsequential word.

Helen Morrow

TWO DEER IN A GLADE

Two deer disturbed, alert to an alien sound,
Tautly aware,
With delicate ears up pointing and forefoot lifted
In the still air,

Then, not once with their great eyes looking
Backward again,
Bound out of the glade, on through the wood, through thicket
    and clearing,
Over the plain.

Not once looking backward, or daring,
At the green glade
Of sunlight, or moonlight, fern bed and small pool,
Or quiet shade.

When speed shortens the breath, when the walls of the heart
    are shaken,
When strangling fingers of fear
Are laid on the throat, and eyes burn in their sockets,
Remember the deer.

Is there no glade with pool for the thirsting and fern for the
    weary,
Safe from the hunter's foot;
Safe from the sound of horns, the baying of lean hounds;
Safe from pursuit;

Must always the hunters halloo and the dogs discover;
Must always the gentle flee from cover to cover?

Pause, eat the willow buds now, my fellow-hunted.
Browse in the glade, and drink from the untroubled stream.
Stand knee deep in the bracken beneath the branches;
The past, a fable all told; the future, a dream.

The forest is full of the breath of the hound and the hunter.
There is no escape.
But all that is past is gone and therefore is powerless; and the
    future
Has not found shape.

This only is real: this moment of sunlight and water,
Aside from the trail.
Though the forest be full of evils pursuing, impending,
For the moment, they fail.

David Morton

PIETIES

I

The flickering lights men live by in the dark:
Pity and love and learning hardly won,
And holy memory pious to remark
Where deeds of thought and deeds of soul were done—
These all are guttering in an evil wind,
And the old darkness takes the world again,
The black wing swoops to cancel and rescind
All we have wrought, and we are stricken men.

This thing has happened to our race before:
The dark, the wind, the dire smoke in the eyes,
The sweet names drowned along the bitter roar,—
And we were saved from those disastrous skies
How but by hands cupped round the assaulted flames,
And lips that moved to form the saving names . . . ?

II

Ambiguous omens throng the angry sky,
And this is midnight in the man's career,
And this the country where all springs are dry
And all his passion gathers to a fear . . .
The dawn, most gracious, when the gods were near,
Wore on to noon, but heaven was too high,
There were too many voices, and none clear—
And this is midnight and the gods gone by.

The man is naked, now, as when he came,
And so alone in darkness east and west,
There are no longer names for him to name,
Save those inviolate ones of his own breast,
Presiding still, when all the gods are gone,
Enthroned within him and decreeing dawn.

Jessie Wilmore Murton

EPITAPH WRITTEN IN SNOW

On this smooth sheet
Of immaculate whiteness,
Small swift feet
Trace a wild thing's lightness:

There is no shape—
Yet the mind, reviewing,
Senses escape,
And a foe, pursuing.

There is no form
For the eye to follow,
Only white norm
Of the hill, and hollow—

Only small prey,
With a pulse like thunder,
Standing at bay . . .
Somewhere . . . out yonder!

Starr Nelson

THE SKELETON ON THE SHORE

After the hurricane the rocky chasms churned
With sea-wrack, and boulders slithery with seaweed shifted
At a touch; but the skeleton the tidal wave had lifted
Upon the ledge drew us as though it burned,

A lode-star, and we two mariners adrift and yearning.
Its bones were as drained of marrow as a shell.
Wind, salt and sun had made them beautiful;
They were white as the dazzling breasts of the seagulls turning
And crying, crying, along this barrier-reef.

What has come over? What have these bones to declare
To vessels whose freight more than the winding worm
Imperils? What hurricanes of blood against belief
They weathered once, or when or where that storm—
Better to ask the gulls, my darling, better to ask the air.

Louise Townsend Nicholl

REFRACTION

Within the mirror of an oval dream
Figures were pictured whitely in a stream.
Water in dream and in the stream reflection;
How much of it was real, how much deflection?
Was beauty blurred, or cameo'd the clearer,
For being seen within the double mirror?
The quivering water-figures as they sank
Were lovelier than those upon the bank.

Image in image toward infinity—
Then in some ultimate mirror would we see
Beauty herself? Or what we wish she were?
Be it herself or only what she seem,
Lovely distortion, still I would prefer
The medium of water and of dream,
Depth within depth to bevel and to bend—
Since I am also one who must depend

On sleep's immersion for my deepest sight
And like a stick in water lean on light.

IN SPACE THE ONE GREAT ORNAMENT

In Space the one great ornament
Of sounds enlaced, coincident,
Three simultaneous tones recur,
And I the only listener . . .
Reverberating through my sleep
From very far, from very deep,
A new creation, new conceived,
A Chord, achieved!

I woke, and it was May and it was morning.
The chime I heard,
The sweet attunèd clash,
Was bird,
Was thrush,
His song my sleep adorning.

Oh, it was heaven to wake and in the waking
Surprise one heaven to another breaking,
To move from world to world so instant near
I carried the eternal in my ear—
A crystal globe meticulously cloven,
Its prismed lusters trembling interwoven,
The phrase immaculate in archetype
From which all consonance derives its shape,
A unity divided then restored
By shards which ring together in a chord.

KNOWING WHAT TIME IT IS AT NIGHT

The night is soundless but its tide has turned—
A candle burning, and a candle burned.
Waking, I listen to the ebbing flood
To sense the still subsidence of its flowing

And marvel at the manner of its going,
As quiet and accustomed as the blood.

No clock records the hour of its height
Nor are there any tide-marks on the night,
Its variance can never be computed.
But its two movements, so intensely muted,
Are simple to distinguish and to know
As are the falling and the fallen snow.

The ear has ancient augury and warning
Of this great tide of time which breaks on morning,
And hungers always toward that outer ocean
Whence time returns, made audible in motion—
The ultimate sound, the silence come to flower,
Which tells the changing and eternal hour.

Grace Fallow Norton

PHOENIX

Reason, and then all
this rancor that I know;
power, and then this pall,
this dread I undergo;

knowledge, a straight flame,
and after, the whirling cloud
of grief, anger and shame;
these, also the proud

the still unspoken high
desire I ponder and how
to cleanse an ardor I
would not disavow.

I would not starve the flame
though it consume my being.
Let it burn my narrow name,
my jangled disagreeing,

burn, burn, till in the ash
cold and fine and pure,
an ember for its flesh
the fabulous bird shall stir.

John Myers O'Hara

ATROPOS

Atropos, dread
One of the Three,
Holding the thread
Woven for me;

Grimly thy shears,
Steely and bright,
Menace the years
Left for delight.

Grant it may chance,
Just as they close,
June may entrance
Earth with the rose;

Reigning as though,
Bliss to the breath,
Endless and no
Whisper of death.

James Oppenheim

TASTING THE EARTH

In a dark hour, tasting the Earth.

As I lay on my couch in the muffled night, and the rain
    lashed my window,
And my forsaken heart would give me no rest, no pause and
    no peace,
Though I turned my face far from the wailing of my
    bereavement,
Then I said: I will eat of this sorrow to its last shred,
I will take it unto me utterly,
I will see if I be not strong enough to contain it.
What do I fear? Discomfort?
How can it hurt me, this bitterness?

The miracle, then!
Turning toward it, and giving up to it,
I found it deeper than my own self . . .
O dark great mother-globe so close beneath me!
It was she with her inexhaustible grief,
Ages of blood-drenched jungles, and the smoking of craters,
    and the roar of tempests,
And moan of the forsaken seas.
It was she with the hills beginning to walk in the shapes
    of the dark-hearted animals,
It was she risen, dashing away tears and praying to dumb skies,
    in the pomp-crumbling tragedy of man.
It was she, container of all griefs, and the buried dust of
    broken hearts,
Cry of the christs and the lovers and the child-stripped mothers,
An ambition gone down to defeat, and the battle overborne,
And the dreams that have no waking . . .

My heart became her ancient heart:
On the food of the strong I fed, on dark strange life itself:
Wisdom-giving and sombre with the unremitting love of ages ...

There was dank soil in my mouth,
And bitter sea on my lips,
In a dark hour, tasting the Earth.

Shaemas O'Sheel

BAGPIPES

I heard the pipes go by
while the low sun silvered the lake,
And I bade my heart be high
for their sake and for your sake,
Since even in this mean day
wild music flung aloud
mocks at the things men say,
and a passionate and proud
young head holds Time at bay.
Beauty stirs in her shroud.

Winthrop Palmer

NEW YORK

This city, all eyes,
Without pity, without surprise
Examines the content of the skies.

Rain, wind nor the snow fearing,
Sand, marsh and river clearing,
Fog, the breath of an ocean, hearing.

Time and tide leave her pale,
A ghostly bride no vows avail,
No season knows, no nightingale.

Her god is hurry; her woman, lacquer;
Her slave, worry; her scribe, a fakir;
Her poet, a commission broker.

She stands before the skies,
This city men prize—
Haggard with merchandise.

Josephine Preston Peabody

CRADLE SONG

I

Lord Gabriel, wilt thou not rejoice
When at last a little boy's
   Cheek lies heavy as a rose,
   And his eyelids close?

Gabriel, when that hush may be,
This sweet hand all heedfully
   I'll undo, for thee alone,
   From his mother's own.

Then the far blue highways paven
With the burning stars of heaven
   He shall gladden with the sweet
   Hasting of his feet—

Feet so brightly bare and cool,
Leaping, as from pool to pool;
    From a little laughing boy
    Splashing rainbow joy!

Gabriel, wilt thou understand
How to keep his hovering hand—
    Never shut, as in a bond,
    From the bright beyond?—

Nay, but though it cling and close
Tightly as a climbing rose,
    Clasp it only so—aright,
    Lest his heart take fright.

(Dormi, dormi, tu:
The dusk is hung with blue.)

II

Lord Michael, wilt thou not rejoice
When at last a little boy's
    Heart, a shut-in murmuring bee,
    Turns him unto thee?

Wilt thou heed thine armor well—
To take his hand from Gabriel,
    So his radiant cup of dream
    May not spill a gleam?

He will take thy heart in thrall,
Telling o'er thy breastplate, all
    Colors, in his bubbling speech,
    With his hand to each.

(Dormi, dormi, tu.
Sapphire is the blue:
Pearl and beryl, they are called
Chrysoprase and emerald,
Sard and amethyst,
Numbered so, and kissed.)

Ah, but find some angel word
For thy sharp, subduing sword!
    Yea, Lord Michael, make no doubt
    He will find it out:

(*Dormi, dormi, tu!*
His eyes will look at you.)

III

Last, a little morning space,
Lead him to that leafy place
    Where Our Lady sits awake,
    For all mothers' sake.

Bosomed with the Blessèd One,
He shall mind her of her Son,
    Once so folded from all harms,
    In her shrining arms.

(*In her veil of blue,*
Dormi, dormi, tu.)

    So;—and fare thee well.
    Softly,—Gabriel . . .
When the first faint red shall come,
Bid the Day-star lead him home,
    For the bright world's sake—
    To my heart, awake.

William Alexander Percy

CONFIDANTS

Rejoice, my heart, that the stars do not comprehend you,
That they march on their mighty courses, serene and terrible,
Unvexed by your sorrow, untarnished by your desires.
You may spread your pain like a purple cloth before them
And their silver and golden feet will brush it lightly
As they brush the cloths of the grass which is more beautiful.
You may cry aloud to them your dolor and desolation,
And though your cry were intolerable and keen as Israfel's,
They would not heed it, high-hearted in the roar of ebbing
    chaos.
Even your self-pity, shining like a gift and shameless,
You may bring them without evil, for they, they only of your
    comrades,
Resist the infection of sorrow, the contagion of tears.

Harold Trowbridge Pulsifer

OF LITTLE FAITH

I said, when the word came, 'She will break
Like a tall ship riven by the shore.'
As a dream, I saw the white sails shake,
The masts fall, heard the smoking combers roar.
I saw the black reef shatter the broken hull,
I saw the dead ship drop from the shore's embrace
And over the empty waters only a screaming gull
Winging its endless way to mark the tragic place.
I felt the blown spume cut like driven snow—
'As a tall ship goes,' I said, 'so she will go!'

I raised my head. I saw her stand
Like a tall ship won home from a gale.
Her eyes like the deep sea far from land
Her white face calm as a sleeping sail.
The touch of her hand was cool as spray,
And her smile like the ripple at the prow
Of a tall ship going its silent way
Through an old swell, quietly breathing now,
After a storm. I said, 'She has shown to me
The deathless glory of the ageless sea.'

Edwin Quarles

THRENODY

Word of her plight is on the wing,
Yet none will give it place so soon:
Never has fared so strange a thing
By sun or moon.

I that should be the last to know
Beheld how certainly and fleet
The loveliest of earth may go
With unreturning feet.

O none will give it place tonight,
Word of her sleeping over-long:
Wait till her rose-tree looks for light,
And her lark goes up for song.

Elizabeth Randall-Mills

THE QUICK STILL CENTER

Sun brightens the mating cardinals,
And sparrow shells fall empty to ground;
Day beginning in the sky
Springs up like a weed; rye,
Ripened, levels the winter galls.

The seed gives to the stem's hour,
The immaculate moment to time—
In its grey-petaled mournful flight
Across the pastures bluet bright
The wild cress acres to deflower.

Summer warms the gourds to grow,
And will, at ending, break them: life
Almost by living overlain.
Trees let go their leaves in rain,
The earth forsakes her grass in snow.

The seasons' coming and retreating
In time, the seed's immediacy,
The quickening center fail to kill:
Be breath in breathing lost, it still
Is source of that airy repeating.

Byron Herbert Reece

WHOSE EYE IS ON THE SPARROW

I saw a fallen sparrow
Dead upon the grass
And mused to see how narrow
The wing that bore it was.

By what unlucky chance
The bird had come to settle
Lop-sided near the fence
In sword grass and nettle

I had no means to know;
But this I minded well:
Whose eye was on the sparrow
Shifted, and it fell.

Lizette Woodworth Reese

IN TIME OF GRIEF

Dark, thinned, beside the wall of stone,
    The box dripped in the air;
Its odor through my house was blown
    Into the chamber there.

Remote and yet distinct the scent,
    The sole thing of its kind,
As though one spoke a word half meant
    That left a sting behind.

I knew not Grief would go from me,
    And naught of it be plain,
Except how keen the box can be
    After a fall of rain.

Cale Young Rice

OLD AGE

I have heard the wild geese,
I have seen the leaves fall,
There was frost last night
On the garden wall.
It is gone today
And I hear the wind call.
The wind? . . . That is all.

If the swallow will light
When the evening is near;
If the crane will not scream
Like a soul in fear;
I will think no more
Of the dying year,
And the wind, its seer.

Rosa Coates Richards

WEAVER

Caught in the growing sweep of that design,
His fingers plied the needle through and through,
Shaping the miracle of form and line,
Each color in its making clear and true.
The weaver watched that testament expand
Into a larger pattern than he thought
Could ever issue from his patient hand,
Wondering at the richness he had wrought.

And so at last the tapestry was done,
Figured with sea and sky and forest green,
Shot through with moonlight, shimmering with sun,
Cities and towns and rivers in between.
He looked upon his labor to behold
Himself the final, gleaming thread of gold.

Margaret R. Richter

ELEGY FOR A LOST CONTINENT

All night long falling from wing-struck air,
The harsh immemorial wild crying blown
Back from the southward bearing long-necked flocks,
Instinct- and autumn-driven their immemorial way.
So pioneers saw them winging; so Audubon saw them,
Wild geese high over river and primeval woodland,
Wildfowl unnumbered seeking the southern marshes,
Hosting of geese in autumn, hosting of geese in spring,
Gray geese flying.

Not alone wild geese hosting, but passenger pigeons,
Multitudes migrating, devouring beechmast;
Tumult of wings and crash of broken branches;
Undulant columns of massed slate-colored bodies,
Thousands on wheeling thousands drawing the wind in their
    wake,
Torrential flying.

In Ohio and Mississippi turkeys assembled,
Spread-tailed marching in flocks toward fertile bottoms,
Old and young on foot, pompously gobbling;
Bronze-plumaged turkeys strutting the woods of October;
Turkeys at night in the trees, head ducked to the owl,
Yellow-eyeballed, wide winged in the moonlight above them;
Shadowbirds dropped from the bough to underwood shelter,
Crouching owl-hidden.

Whooping canes on grass-grown reaches of prairie,
Birds of the lonely horizon and untrodden marshland,
Long white lines on the stormy wind of November;
Snow-winged circling the meadow, long-legged alighting,
Shaking their feathers, proudly stalking the lakeside;
Wary, outrunning the deer, spiralling upward,
Winding and cying.

Always the Indian summer, always the hosting
Down the wide valley through immemorial autumn,
The hosting of life in the continent of the red man;
Always the turning of maple and gum, the falling of oakleaves,
Always the migrating wildfowl, the pioneer memory
Of prodigal wild life on the primitive continent,
Gone from the ploughfield.

We have lived too long out of reach of wolf and cougar;
Insensitive to living itself, men live;
Within them the strong disregarding of life, inherent defect
Sunk deep in a civilization reared to destroy,
Self-annihilating this moment, reckoning equal
Mankind and wildfowl.

Always the Indian summer, the wild geese flying,
America crying—an immemorial crying—
Free-pinioned crying,
Down the long valley of time;
Crying a white-winged morrow.

Jessie B. Rittenhouse

THE HAWTHORN

The hawthorn in the Devon lanes
Is white upon the tree
As I ride down to Lynmouth,
Beloved of you and me.

For I remember that in youth
You too had wandered here,
And walked the lanes of Devon
And held the hawthorn dear;

And I am overtaken
By pain all pain above,
For what can smite like beauty
That is not shared by love?

Clyde Robertson

THE YELLOW WITCH OF CARIBOU

The hills are high in Caribou,
The air is clear—the skies are blue;
But where a black ledge seams the ground
The yellow witch's tracks are found
And men grow drunk with ravishment
Once they have caught the witch's scent.

The aspens on the mountain side
Were green when Carlo brought his bride,
The cherry-cheeked Selina, to
The haunted hills of Caribou.

"You better take your man and go,"
The old wives warned, "before the snow;
The yellow witch hides in these hills
And gets our men against their wills."

Selina shook her bold, black head,
"My Carlo will not leave my bed
To hammer on a speckled door
A huntin' any yellow whore;
He's signed up with the sawmill crew,
He's safe enough in Caribou.

"Who minds the talk of wrinkled crones,
Their skin a stickin' to their bones—
Their men folks might go trailin' round
A chasin' witch tracks in the ground;
But *my* man's *mine!* I'm not afraid
I'll lose him to a stealin' jade.
"Child, we were all the same as you,
When we were brought to Caribou.

We know, as only old wives can,
The curse of havin' half a man.
We know the end of these old tracks—
The blinded eyes—and broken backs."

But when the mountain side grew red
And pulsing as a wanton's bed
Young Carlo's eyes flamed with the fire
Of an unhallowed, mad desire.
Selina knew his passion meant
"Her man" had caught the witch's scent.
Before the first snow veiled the crest
Like lace upon a woman's breast
She saw him leave the sheltering mills
To roam among the siren hills.
But no man yet has come to know
Which way the yellow witch may go;
She burrows deep in porphyry rocks
And bars her trail with granite blocks.
So Carlo did as all men do
That chase the witch of Caribou.

At last upon a sloping crest,
As rounded as a woman's breast,
Beneath a snow of winding lace
He tracked her to her hiding place.
Here, in an evil, blackened niche,
He mated with the yellow witch.

At dawn Selina found him there
Strangled, by a golden hair.

Edwin Arlington Robinson

FLAMMONDE

The man Flammonde, from God knows where,
With firm address and foreign air,
With news of nations in his talk
And something royal in his walk,
With glint of iron in his eyes,
But never doubt, nor yet surprise,
Appeared, and stayed, and held his head
As one by kings accredited.

Erect, with his alert repose
About him, and about his clothes,
He pictured all tradition hears
Of what we owe to fifty years.
His cleansing heritage of taste
Paraded neither want nor waste;
And what he needed for his fee
To live, he borrowed graciously.

He never told us what he was,
Or what mischance, or other cause,
Had banished him from better days
To play the Prince of Castaways.
Meanwhile he played surpassing well
A part, for most, unplayable;
In fine, one pauses, half afraid
To say for certain that he played.

For that, one may as well forego
Conviction as to yes or no;
Nor can I say just how intense
Would then have been the difference
To several, who, having striven
In vain to get what he was given,

Would see the stranger taken on
By friends not easy to be won.

Moreover, many a malcontent
He soothed and found munificent;
His courtesy beguiled and foiled
Suspicion that his years were soiled;
His mien distinguished any crowd,
His credit strengthened when he bowed;
And women, young and old, were fond
Of looking at the man Flammonde.

There was a woman in our town
On whom the fashion was to frown;
But while our talk renewed the tinge
Of a long-faded scarlet fringe,
The man Flammonde saw none of that,
And what he saw we wondered at—
That none of us, in her distress,
Could hide or find our littleness.

There was a boy that all agreed
Had shut within him the rare seed
Of learning. We could understand,
But none of us could lift a hand.
The man Flammonde appraised the youth,
And told a few of us the truth;
And thereby, for a little gold,
A flowered future was unrolled.

There were two citizens who fought
For years and years, and over nought;
They made life awkward for their friends,
And shortened their own dividends.
The man Flammonde said what was wrong
Should be made right, nor was it long
Before they were again in line,
And had each other in to dine.

And these I mention are but four
Of many out of many more.
So much for them. But what of him—
So firm in every look and limb?
What small satanic sort of kink
Was in his brain? What broken link
Withheld him from the destinies
That came so near to being his?

What was he, when we came to sift
His meaning, and to note the drift
Of incommunicable ways
That make us ponder while we praise?
Why was it that his charm revealed
Somehow the surface of a shield?
What was it that we never caught?
What was he, and what was he not?

How much it was of him we met
We cannot ever know; nor yet
Shall all he gave us quite atone
For what was his, and his alone;
Nor need we now, since he knew best,
Nourish an ethical unrest:
Rarely at once will nature give
The power to be Flammonde and live.

We cannot know how much we learn
From those who never will return,
Until a flash of unforeseen
Remembrance falls on what has been.
We've each a darkening hill to climb;
And that is why, from time to time
In Tilbury Town, we look beyond
Horizons for the man Flammonde.

Henry Morton Robinson

WEEK-END LOVE

In rooms too-often let, too-meanly furnished,
Do we, my love, pale Saturday refugees,
Find dusty silence waiting to be burnished
By transient hands to joy in fugitive keys;
Through curtained Sundays while the hired dream hovers
Above our foreheads in a pitying spell,
Have we not roamed, a pair of happy lovers,
Wall-papered heavens in a cheap hotel?

Something between a secret and a boast
Lies on our lips in parting at the corner;
Something, once found, that never can be lost,
Something that needs both celebrant and mourner,
Telling us that we are, (oh shabby doom)
Poor week-end lovers in a rented room.

SECOND WISDOM

Corn does not hurry, and the black grape swells
In the slow cadence of all ripening things;
Wise pumpkins idle, and the deep lake dwells
In peace above her unimpetuous springs.

What most unhurried, most full-flavorous is:
The earth turns slowly and the tide stands still
For him who surely claims, as truly his,
Firm fruitage that no hasty blight can kill.

And we who flung ourselves to sudden wars
And would not wait for quick scars to be healed—
We must recall shrewd pumpkins and slow stars
And be as wise as lilies of the field.

James Rorty

THE BELL-RINGERS

In the dark days, the early evenings of December,
With summer gone, and autumn, and the pale towers of the
    skyscrapers withered in the high cold, or blind in rain,
And the people stumbling home, sick with small fears, the little
    lies of trade, the multiple loneliness of crowds,
Then the Christmas bell-ringers come forth, the mute whiskered
    false-faces, each with his iron kettle and his bell.
Ting-ling-ling, ting-ling-ling—how hesitant, how humble these
    priests; is something really born, are they sure?
Long ago the desert villagers heard this bell; then the tired
    Greeks, the Romans, even the reindeer people of the
    north—all fed the myth and the myth sustained them.
By this faith the pale towers rise, the myriad lights burn, the
    shoaled motors race and stop, overhead a great ship drills
    a lighted wake through the new ocean of the night air.
One small scrap of ancient holiness—out of this we have built
    a world unholy, terrible and fierce; but we are neither
    fierce nor terrible.
The blood of the lamb grows thin; next year or next century
    will the bell-ringers come again to the street corners?
Not for long shall we dream this dream when fierceness wakes
    again in our blood we shall want not bells, but trumpets,
    and again the high cross.

END OF FARCE

The play ends. Children, go home.
Go home, children, the bright tree is dark, there are no good
    fairies.
On tip-toe, children, steal home, hush, be grave.
Hide, children, in the damp cellars, the Pharaoh has marked
    the door-posts.

Rain, rain, on the far horizon, light, fierce light, and the deep
    wing roaring.

Go home, children. Children, go home.

Change like a vomit, change like a vast labor spewing forth
The small souls, the shrill greeds, the thin small rages of
    children.
This wide land aches with the little idiot laughters of children.
Silence, you brats, you misbegotten! Be still, time will not wait,
    the deep wind rises.
Go home, children, hide, weep, you must die, you must be born
    again.

Go home, children. Children, go home.

What shall we do, great Mother, since man must live?
What shall we do between ice and ice?
What shall we do, so loud the locust whines?
How shall they march, the spoiled, the craven, the blind?

They shall march.

How shall they hear us who have not heard
The Bacchae singing at the gates?

They shall hear.

How shall they see us who have not seen
The fierce Valkyrie riding on the wind?

*They shall see, they shall hear, they shall march, and you shall
    weep.
The play ends. The play begins. Not yours, not yours.
Go home, children. Children, go home.*

Coleman Rosenberger

A MEMORIAL FOR MR. JEFFERSON

The white marble stands among the mosquitoes
And Mr. Jefferson is not here.
The monstrous Jefferson, like papier maché
Three times life, leans from the Potomac
And the poll tax.

The Jacobin shadow falls
Upon the picnickers and their Sunday boats.
Buried under the columns, the masonry,
Is the dream of fitting government
And the happy state.

This does you no service, good citizen
Who drew your own so modest monument.
Your words, chosen as carefully as the boxwood,
Buttress the memorial where Mr. Smythe
May lay his wreath.

The interior, domed, and the portico
The plaza, the house in caricature—
Here once more is the silly Browere
Striking the features of the face
That he would keep.

David Ross

BROADCAST TO THE SCHOLARS IN THE EYRIE

Eagles, leave your sky
Of mummied air
To the embalmer's care
Or curator's catalog;
Serve no more with idolatry
The monastic stratosphere;
The crag, cowled in fog.

Shatter the glacial trance
That grips in cataleptic vise
The blood's circumstance;
Thaw out the compassionate marrow
In the brothering air
Of residential skies
Tenanted by man and sparrow.

Now time is germinal
With pods of bursting days,
Whose air is crucial
With magnetic loyalties;
Man bursts his private shore of skin;
His pulses liberate their tides
To wider commonwealths;
Eagles, lift your quarantine.

Now is cock-crow to torpid suns
Pillowed in the mind;
Antennaed light runs
Tendrils to the earth. The blind
Who fingered life with braille,
Now drink the world with sight.

Eagles, spread sail!
Leave the glacial seas
For your just home and kin;
Declare your blood's allegiance
As lover and citizen.

Sydney King Russell

INVOCATION

Moon of the lost season, linger near,
Moon of returning autumn, heed again
The heart's cry over the lonely weir,
The heart's shadow dark upon the plain.

See how the hare is furtive in the grasses,
The cricket's song is stilled, the plaintive loon
Withholds his call. Time trembles as he passes—
The rose will droop, its petals fall too soon.

Moon of remembrance, turn, but not for long,
Mirror this rapture delicate and brief.
Moon of the lost season, be my song,
My comfort in the night of unbelief.

I. L. Salomon

FIT REMEMBRANCE

I should not want the quarried slate
Or granite to perpetuate
My memory when I am gone.

It is not fit. I fought with stone
Too long to have its weight upon
The locked earth underneath whose sod
I measure less than half a rod.

To know I was may my bones be
Tied to the anonymity
Of hidden roots so intertwined
The man I was becomes defined
In one tall maple tree whose shade
Falls gratefully where I am laid.

Harriet Sampson

FREEDOM CONSIDERED

Freedom, considered, seems to be
Only another boundary,

And liberty a picket fence
With one small gate of common sense

And pointed palings of control
Marking the meadow of the soul.

And if in time my fence and gate
Seem insolent and obdurate,

And if rebelliously I lean
Over the gate or look between

The palings and grow keen for some
Unending jaunt to Kingdom Come,

I shall remember in my wrath
I set the posts, I nailed the lath,

And built this sturdy fence to be
My own preferred austerity.

George Santayana

ODE TO MEDITERRANEAN

Of thee the Northman by his beached galley
Dreamt, as he watched the never-setting Ursa
And longed for summer and thy light, O sacred
    Mediterranean.

Unseen he loved thee; for the heart within him
Knew earth had gardens where he might be blessed,
Putting away long dreams and aimless, barbarous
    Hunger for battle.

The foretaste of thy languors thawed his bosom;
A great need drove him to thy caverned islands
From the gray, endless reaches of the outer
    Desert of ocean.

He saw thy pillars, saw thy sudden mountains
Wrinkled and stark, and in their crooked gorges,
'Neath peeping pine and cypress, guessed the torrent
    Smothered in flowers.

Thine incense to the sun, thy gathered vapours,
He saw suspended on the flanks of Taurus,
Or veiling the snowed bosom of the virgin
    Sister of Atlas.

He saw the luminous top of wide Olympus,
Fit for the happy gods; he saw the pilgrim
River, with rains of Ethiopia flooding
    Populous Egypt.

And having seen, he loved thee. His racked spirit,
By thy breath tempered and the light that clothes thee,
Forgot the monstrous gods, and made of Nature
    Mistress and mother.

The more should I, O fatal sea, before thee
Of alien words make echoes to thy music;
For I was born where first the rills of Tagus
    Turn to the westward,

And wandering long, alas! have need of drinking
Deep of the patience of thy perfect sadness,
O thou that constant through the change of ages,
    Beautiful ever,

Never wast wholly young and void of sorrows,
Nor ever canst be old, while yet the morning
Kindles thy ripples, or in the golden evening
    Dyes thee in purple.

Thee, willing to be tamed but still untamable,
The Roman called his own until he perished,
As now the busy English hover o'er thee,
    Stalwart and noble;

But all is nought to thee, while no harsh winter
Congeals thy fountains, and thy blown Sahara
Chokes not with dreadful sand thy deep and placid
    Rock-guarded havens.

Thou carest not what men may tread thy margin;
Nor I, while from some heather-scented headland
I may behold thy beauty, the eternal
    Solace of mortals.

O WORLD

O world, thou choosest not the better part!
It is not wisdom to be only wise,
And on the inward vision close the eyes,
But it is wisdom to believe the heart.

Columbus found a world, and had no chart,
Save one that faith deciphered in the skies;
To trust the soul's invincible surmise
Was all his science and his only art.
Our knowledge is a torch of smoky pine
That lights the pathway but one step ahead
Across a void of mystery and dread.
Bid, then, the tender light of faith to shine
By which alone the mortal heart is led
Unto the thinking of the thought divine.

Lew Sarett

TO A WILD GOOSE OVER DECOYS

O lonely trumpeter, coasting down the sky,
Like a winter leaf blown from the bur-oak tree
By whipping winds, and flapping silverly
Against the sun—I know your lonely cry.

I know the worn wild heart that bends your flight
And circles you above this beckoning lake,
Eager of neck, to find the honking drake
Who speaks of reedy refuge for the night.

I know the sudden rapture that you fling
In answer to our friendly gander's call—
Halloo! Beware decoys!—or you will fall
With a silver bullet whistling in your wing!

Beat on your weary flight across the blue!
Beware, O traveller, of our gabbling geese!
Beware this weedy counterfeit of peace! . . .
Oh, I was once a passing bird like you.

CATTLE BELLS

How clear tonight the far jang-jangling bells
Of Champlain's herd, the melody that wells
Tuneful as stony water, from the nook
    In the sweet-grass marsh of Alder Brook.

What patient strength of earth their tones disclose:
The peace of stars like quiet-falling snows,
Of forests slumbering, soundless, but for the fox
    Stepping among the clinking rocks.

What world unsullied, free of guile and snare,
What valley of contentment they declares:
A valley soothing as its bullfrog croak,
    Serene as the one slim drifting smoke;

A valley of waters that softly talk of dreams,
Of the slow sweet enterprises of little streams,
Of their solemn concern with every woodland thing
    Lingering to bathe a paw, a wing;

Of the veery, thick with sleep, who stretched his throat
And tossed in the brook a single pebbly note;
Of the frothing doe who buried her muzzle, drank
    And dropped in the brookmints on the bank . . .

I shall lie down and sleep . . . sleep now . . .
And yield to the cool bells this blazing brow—
Knowing grief will not stalk me, nor intrude
    Longer tonight upon my brood.

Now that the placid bells have given birth
To the gentle certainties of night and earth,
I shall lie down and sleep, sleep tranquilly;
    And trouble, trouble will fall from me.

FOUR LITTLE FOXES

Speak gently, Spring, and make no sudden sound;
For in my windy valley, yesterday I found

New-born foxes squirming on the ground—
    Speak gently.

Walk softly, March, forbear the bitter blow;
Her feet within a trap, her blood upon the snow,
The four little foxes saw their mother go—
    Walk softly.

Go lightly, Spring, oh, give them no alarm;
When I covered them with boughs to shelter them from harm,
The thin blue foxes suckled at my arm—
    Go lightly.

Step softly, March, with your rampant hurricane;
Nuzzling one another, and whimpering with pain,
The new little foxes are shivering in the rain—
    Step softly.

John Schaffner

AN ISLAND

In this world, O scattered man,
seek out an island, if you can;
build house of stone upon its shore
near enough the ocean's roar
not to feel too safe therein.—
And then remember where you've been.
And then remember where you are.

Keep your island like a star.

Clinton Scollard

"AS I CAME DOWN FROM LEBANON"

As I came down from Lebanon,
Came winding, wandering slowly down
Through mountain-passes bleak and brown,
The cloudless day was well-nigh done.
The city, like an opal, set
In emerald, showed each minaret
Afire with radiant beams of sun,
And glistened orange, fig, and lime,
Where song-birds made melodious chime,
As I came down from Lebanon.

As I came down from Lebanon,
Like lava in the dying glow,
Through olive orchards far below
I saw the murmuring river run;
And 'neath the wall upon the sand
Swart sheiks from distant Samarcand,
With precious spices they had won,
Lay long and languidly in wait
Till they might pass the guarded gate,
As I came down from Lebanon.

As I came down from Lebanon,
I saw strange men from lands afar,
In mosque and square and gay bazar,
The Magi that the Moslem shun,
And grave Effendi from Stamboul,
Who sherbet sipped in corners cool;
And, from the balconies o'errun
With roses, gleamed the eyes of those
Who dwell in still seraglios,
As I came down from Lebanon.

As I came down from Lebanon,
The flaming flower of daytime died,
And Night, arrayed as is a bride
Of some great king, in garments spun
Of purple and the finest gold,
Outbloomed in glories manifold!
Until the moon, above the dun
And darkening desert, void of shade,
Shone like a keen Damascus blade,
As I came down from Lebanon.

Anderson M. Scruggs

MAN IS FOREVER LONELY

Man is forever lonely; there can be
No time or circumstance in all his days
To lead him out of loneliness. His ways
Are those of clouds and tides. Not even he
Who seeks the crowded solace of the street
Can find a single comrade there, nor yet
In secret bonds of love can men forget
Their heart's own solitude. Though lips may meet
And hand touch hand in intimate embrace,
A stranger still abides within the mind
No word can reach, no vision ever find.
A lonely God, enthroned in lonely space,
Fashioned us out of silence as we are:
As single as a tree, as separate as a star.

Frank Dempster Sherman

BACCHUS

Listen to the tawny thief,
Hid beneath the waxen leaf,
Growling at his fair host,
Bidding her with angry boast
Fill his cup with wine distilled
From the dew the dawn has spilled:
Stored away in golden casks
Is the precious draught he asks.

Who,—who makes this mimic din
In this mimic meadow inn,
Sings in such a drowsy note,
Wears a golden-belted coat;
Loiters in the dainty room
Of this tavern of perfume;
Dares to linger at the cup
Till the yellow sun is up?

Bacchus 'tis, come back again
To the busy haunts of men;
Garlanded and gaily dressed,
Bands of gold about his breast;
Straying from his paradise,
Having pinions angel-wise,—
'Tis the honey-bee who goes
Reveling within a rose!

Ruth Forbes Sherry

CORONAL: A LEGEND OF THE ANNUNCIATION

Gentian blue as noon-lit sea
　　Was Mary's gown of blue.
She smoothed her kerchief carefully
　　As women do.

The angel knelt, his wings downbent,
　　His gold hair paved the ground.
And Mary knew whence he was sent,
　　And made no sound.

Far out beyond the farthest star
　　She heard a silver singing.
Gloria in Excelsis—far
　　And farther ringing.

She took the lily in her hand
　　Wondering what it meant,
And seemed almost to understand
　　The white intent.

A coronal of sea-deep thought
　　Sat royally on her brow,
The simple prayers that she was taught
　　Forgotten now.

And from her face so deep a light
　　Spilled out it was as though
Creation wrapped her round with bright
　　Prophetic glow.

And Gabriel slipped into the gloom
　　And tip-toed up the sky.
And no one entered Mary's room
　　Or heard her sigh.

And Mary knew the fire-flower
   Close within her womb.
And down the years, the flaming hour—
   The empty tomb.

Constance Lindsay Skinner

INDIAN SPRING

I on the thighs of God, as the leaf on the willow!
I the song of his lips and the light of his mirth,
I the wind between his frontlets, the desire to his children,
I the sure arrow of his heart!

I the drums of his walking where the mountains roll the echo,
I the bellying mist on his seas that sail the world;
I the speech of his rivers to the stark and silent places,
I the chant of his stars, descending through the dark to the
    sea-call,
I the reedy flutes of his peace!

I the wings of his cliffs, thrilling to the morning,
I the carol of his cloud-gnomes leaping through the moon,
I the mild content of his slow, waddling, sniffing bear;
I the dartle of his sands, I the gossip of his fishes
'Neath the coast where his ancient bearded cedars lie a-snoring
    in the breeze.
I the goodwill of his sun, I the dew of his promise,
I the gratitude of the small, sweet grass!

I the seed in his spilling pouches, I the spear that wounds to
    harvest;
I the life-bringer, I his servant to the law that is forever;
I the linked hands of unborn children—

Mystic fetter round the loins of men and women;
I the sober splendor of their fusion, I the paean of their hope!
Oh, I on the thighs of God, as the leaf on the willow!

Eleanor Sands Smith

DEATH STIRS THE ARRAS

The little lamp that lit my room
Cast a light that they named doom.

My stillness caused their blood to freeze,
They crossed their breasts, fell on their knees.

They thought because I had no breath
That I had gone away with death.

The night was cold, wolves sought the pack,
And water stumbled in its track.

They called me back to life again
With quick-sand love, and cursed amen.

But I could damn their souls to hell
Who prayed for me and wished me well.

*From chaos to chaos, I had played
In purple light and spiced fern shade;*

*My high-arched feet had left designs
Along where ran the russet hinds;*

*A fox led by my golden belt,
For love of me, beside me knelt,*

*Nuzzling me with the satin sheath
That held the fury of his teeth.*

Staccato barks I think I hear,
But know him dead long since from fear . . .

Quiet now from summer trips
To hunt for fruits to stain my lips!

For us no more the green-cressed creek
Where currants hung for us to seek . . .

And never, never the merry horn
Winding through the white rose-thorn.

Leonora Speyer

THESE POEMS I HAVE SO LOVED

Reading them over and over,
The books of deathless song
Scattered about my bed,
Each with its wide-stretched cover:
These are the friend, the lover.

Poems I have loved the best;
Holding their page to the light,
I read them, call them aloud,
Craving no deeper rest,
Than an open book on my breast.

Thus at the end—and lying
As I lie now with their words,
These poems I have so loved,
Their voices, vast, undying,
And my small voice replying.

NOTE TO 'FIDDLER'S FAREWELL'

I held a fiddle in my hand again,
Under my chin I tucked the tameless wood,
And it was good.

I made no sound, nor did I lay the bow
To the four strings; only the fingers pressed
With their old zest.

Only the violin (that box of birds!)
Sensed the blurred notes, the fingers' urgency,
Fugitive, shy:

Laughed—and flung music free, as if a door;
I entered the rich room,
And I was home.

THE WEEPER

Who is weeping in the apartment above?
I have heard the long-winged sea-birds in the solitary air
(As querulous, as shrill),
But there was sunlight mixed with their crying,
And this is in the night.

This sound is a dark blade
Cutting harsh patterns of grief—
Silhouette of a woman weeping.

I hear no words,
But how explicit is this idiom,
This blurred derivative of language:
Here is a tale full-throated,
A disheveled, noisy sorrow
Coarsely and pitifully told;
Anguish is the common tongue all speak,
And the listener, however reluctant,
Must bear witness.

Through my ceiling,
Through the ceiling of night,
Stretches this high whimpering,
Taut as steel wire,
On which the violent heart careens and teeters—
Crazed tightrope walker
About to fall.

Lawrence Perry Spingarn

ROCOCO SUMMER

After split skies and tardy thunder, rain
Recalled the children in their pinafores
To porches tense with sportsmen. Bores
Peddled the myth of Vicksburg once again.
Grant himself, bribed with a fine cigar,
Sinister, taciturn, sick with his cancer,
Snatched from a silver tray the cabled answer,
Read he would die, smiled, headed for the bar.
The sky protested. Mallets clicked dismay.
Beneath wet elms the darkey waiters served
Tall, minted juleps. Sudden horsemen swerved,
Missing a child, reining another way.
The sun returned. Oh, what is left to tell?
No pen stabs reputation. From the lawn,
Duly escorted, not without a yawn,
Women moved gravely toward the dinner bell.

Florence Dickinson Stearns

BARGAIN

Since you are gone,
Eternity begins,
(Beware old sins)
I had forgot
That Atropos still claims the spot
Where life removes its cloak and shoon
In unimpeded afternoon.
Forgotten too, so deep my love,
That loss and sacrifice will move
The heavenly host
To grant an unprotected ghost
Convoy from here,
And so I clear
This prudent hour
To bargain for an acre
Of the Ultimate. Partaker
Of smooth security I'll be;
The purchase price
A single memory.

Forgetting is a royal thing:
Not vassal like remembering.

George Sterling

PARIS

Far-off he heard upon the truce of night
    The wail of kindred women for their slain;
    Far-off he saw across the shrouding rain

The foeman's leaguer, arrogant with light,
And turned to where, inimically bright,
    Her beauty burned immaculate of stain.
    Yea! it was worth the hatreds and the pain,
The gleaming ranks disastrous in the fight!

This thing was of the ages. This was she
For whom the nations gathered as a sea
That foamed in death, and ebbing, left a wrack
    Of swords and helms, of chariots and spears,
    And, on the red horizon of the years,
The memory of sails that come not back.

Helen Frith Stickney

FROM AN IVORY TOWER

An ivory tower leans against the wind,
The wind of space;
It is not built by toil nor discplined
By time or place.

For here the merging mists are pinnacled
With upright grace,
There is a sound of rushing echoes, thinned
Beyond all trace;
And dawn lies cool, perpetual, on the wind,
The wind of space.

A. M. Sullivan

THE CHRONOMETER

"What time is it?" said the one,
"Whose time do you want?" said the second
Holding a stick in the sun
To see what the shadow reckoned.

"What time is it by the moon?"
Said another beside the Deep
And the salt winds answered "Soon,
For there are Tides to keep."

And they asked a sailor the time
And he answered loud and rude
"Go count the bells that chime
On the lines of longitude."

And they asked a saint to tell
The time for the bended knee
And he said "In Heaven and Hell,
Who measures Eternity?"

But they asked no beast the season
Of love and birth and fear
For Death plays all things treason
In any time of year.

The clepsydra counts by water
The glass by the falling sand,
The dame by her blooming daughter,
The jade by her withered hand.

Who cares for the time of the stars
Where the pendulum swings an arc
From the dusk of the dinosaurs
To the dawn in Menlo Park?

Listen for the tick and tock
As the mainspring's gathered strength
Uncoils within the clock
And measures a day's full length,

And hark to the echo's sound
After the cannon cease
And put your lips to the ground
And whisper "The time is Peace."

COUNSEL FOR YOUTH

Let not the white, hot metal of your desire
Chill under the breath of scorn;
Before the dream dies, gather the bitter briar
And watch the flames leap higher
Making a golden fagot of every thorn.

Drink your rapture before the blood thickens,
In bulging and brittle veins;
Sire your phantoms while the pulse quickens,
Else the spirit sickens
And the rainbow drips from unwoven skeins.

Fling your golden pennies to the intrepid dancers
Who spin on the point of swords,
And borrow the red shawl of the necromancers
Or, all your lyric answers
Will crumble into words.

Elda Tanasso

MORNING WITHOUT MALICE

The star went quiet like a sunken bell.
Chastely, and more an abstract thought now spreading,

The less star-troubled and tree-lined, the sky
Moves over the small place where my enemy fell,

Where all around in soft and sweet disguise
Woodflowers stand, the crocus and the sage,
Remote from terror in me who have seen
A comrade watching from my enemy's eyes.

This harmony of morning and white space
And sound of distance on approaching wind
Sharpens the discord that I struck when blind
To the keen sorrow in my enemy's face.

The sun breaks slowly where the thin hills lean
Westward, southward, seaward. Enemy
Was comrade with a soft, familiar voice,
And I a comrade with my blade wiped clean.

Anne Southerne Tardy

SUN THROUGH WINDOW SHUTTERS

This casual sunlight breaking through with proud
Effrontery, disregarding a pierced shield,
Could, unobstructed by a blind or cloud,
Mete fire to men or oxen in a field.

As undulating as the wind upon the pool
From which it is reflected, it has all
The salutary movement of the cool
Bright willows, pendulous by the water-fall.

Beware oh heart! This treacherous bland light
Which journeys whisperless across the floor,
Moves with authority, marking the flight
Of radiant hours no hand may restore.

Mary Atwater Taylor

THE LITTLE PROGRESS

The snail's small fog-grey silhouette
Inches along the April bough
Slow-paced and steady, definite . . .
Behold him now
As, without aid of speed or wing,
The patience of his shell is borne
Through the green tunnels of the spring
To rest upon the thorn.

Sara Teasdale

ARCTURUS IN AUTUMN

When, in the gold October dusk, I saw you near to setting,
    Arcturus, bringer of spring,
Lord of the summer nights, leaving us now in autumn,
    Having no pity on our withering;

Oh then I knew at last that my own autumn was upon me,
    I felt it in my blood,
Restless as dwindling streams that still remember
    The music of their flood.

There in the thickening dark a wind-bent tree above me
    Loosed its last leaves in flight—
I saw you sink and vanish, pitiless Arcturus,
    You will not stay to share our lengthening night.

Rosemary Thomas

NEW HAMPSHIRE

Five elms as solid underneath as over
prove the earth before his dusty house,
elms that were not much bigger than the clover
when he was not much bigger than a mouse
have put on forty feet of trunk since then,—
richly naked, half the year in snow,
planted against the north, until again
hot streams of sun unbrittle every bough.
These are his trees, his piece of earth, his place,
his two impatient horses stamp the barn,
hungry for his lean New England face,—
too old for work, but twitching for a yarn
from that low voice, so plain a kinship lies
within the sharp blue harbor of his eyes.

Dorothy Brown Thompson

IN TIME OF SNOW

There is no privacy in time of snow.
Here lovers passed the clearing, two and two,
Big prints and small, a good eight hours ago.

There in the field are marks in threes, made new
By night-bold rabbits underneath the moon;
Here by the fence is where the dog slipped through

Wriggling past broken rails. These traces soon
Will be erased. Look quickly, for the sun
Like a stern censor, long before the noon

Will hush the news the while it is begun.
Even the lace designs where the birds' feet go
Will be wiped out—the white swift tale be done.

Look quickly then, or you may never know;
There is no privacy in time of snow.

Eunice Tietjens

THE MOST-SACRED MOUNTAIN

Space, and the twelve clean winds of heaven,
And this sharp exultation, like a cry, after the slow six thousand
    steps of climbing!
This is Tai Shan, the beautiful, the most holy.

Below my feet the foot-hills nestle, brown with flecks of green;
    and lower down the flat brown plain, the floor of earth,
    stretches away to blue infinity.
Beside me in this airy space the temple roofs cut their slow
    curves against the sky,
And one black bird circles above the void.

Space, and the twelve clean winds are here;
And with them broods eternity—a swift, white peace, a presence
    manifest.
The rhythm ceases here. Time has no place. This is the end that
    has no end.

Here, when Confucius came, a half a thousand years before the
    Nazarene, he stepped, with me, thus into timelessness.

The stone beside us waxes old, the carven stone that says: "On
   this spot once Confucius stood and felt the smallness of the
   world below."
The stone grows old:
Eternity is not for stones.
But I shall go down from this airy place, this swift white peace,
   this stinging exultation.

And time will close about me, and my soul stir to the rhythm of
   the daily round.
Yet, having known, life will not press so close, and always I shall
   feel time ravel thin about me;
For once I stood
In the white windy presence of eternity.

Ridgely Torrence

HARVEST HOME

Leave the thirsting cattle,
Leave the standing grain,
Go and win the battle,
Go and heap the slain.

That's the daring labor
For the richer yield:
Neighbor reaping neighbor
In the trampled field.

Reap with will to bind it,
Reap through flesh and bone.
Find the life behind it,
Reaper, is your own.

When the foe is scattered,
Time will heap the cost,
And the victor, shattered,
Know that he has lost.

PROTHALAMIUM
(*To a bride in war time*)

Now the doom on land and sea
    Lengthens toward the wedding day,
Let the bridal bravely be
    Though the world should burn away.

Face, with phoenix wings unfurled,
    Deepening ashes, towering pyre.
Rise above a ruined world
    With a more than mortal fire.

Speed the mating, crown the vow
    While the brand of havoc gleams.
Now's the time to mate and now
    Breed the men with better dreams.

THREE O'CLOCK
(*Morning*)

The jewel-blue electric flowers
    Are cold upon their iron trees.
Upraised, the deadly harp of rails
    Whines for its interval of ease.
The stones keep all their daily speech
    Buried, but can no more forget
Than would a water-vacant beach
    The hour when it was wet.

A whitened few wane out like moons,
    Ghastly from some torn edge of shade;
A drowning one, a reeling one,
    And one still loitering after trade.

On high the candor of a clock
  Portions the darks with solemn sound.
The burden of the bitten rock
  Moans up from underground.

For down the street a shutting door
  Echoes the yesterday that fled
Among the days that should have been
  Which people cities of the dead.
The banners of the steam unfold
  Upon the towers to meet the day;
The lights go out in red and gold
  But time goes out in gray.

Charles Hanson Towne

OF ONE SELF-SLAIN

When he went blundering back to God,
  His songs half written, his work half done,
Who knows what paths his bruised feet trod,
  What hills of peace or pain he won?

I hope God smiled, and took his hand,
  And said, "Poor truant, passionate fool!
Life's book is hard to understand;
  Why couldst thou not remain at school?"

Virginia Lyne Tunstall

APRIL'S DAUGHTER
(Lizette Woodworth Reese, 1856-1935)

How far, how far are you faring, April's daughter?
    When will you turn, turn and come home again?
Listen—the rumour of the spring is whispered
    Along the loneliest lane.

Cherry and plum will powder the grass with stardust,
    The thin white petals riding the scarce stirred air.
Sweet as a chime, its rose before the roses
    The apple tree will bear.

Swift, swift to their clear and silvery conclusions
    The fleeting days of sun and shower will run.
Briefest of things beloved are spring's bright moments
    Before her setting sun.

Lilac and daffodil are yours, yours to remember,
    Though splendoured the eternity you roam.
Ah, delicately drifts the news of April.
    When will you come home?

Jean Starr Untermeyer

UNSHARED ELEGY

There will be none to chronicle the event,
No one to say a word of you or me
When we shall die of how our lives were spent
Or how much love was spilled between us three;

Remember nothing will be said,
No one is left for weeping or for care,
No guardian of truth, no heart to dare—
The Chronicler is dead!

The little eaglet—how far has he flown
Who dreamed of bearing to the crags of sky
His infant-forebears till they should have grown
Fit for the starry road he traveled by.
From what strange conflict was he bred,
And why in its last battle was he caught—
This agony of asking answers naught—
The Chronicler is dead!

Let May burst on the world with new green fire,
October flicker to a ruddy ash,
Neither the resurrection of desire
Nor the reluctant phoenix in that flash
His embered heart throws on his head
Shall be recorded by the loving hand;
There is no advocate in all the land—
The Chronicler is dead!

Now bitterness is bettered by despair
That must go silent to an unsung grave.
Was my heart tuned to courage, was I fair?
Were you the lord of passion or the knave?
No pious memoirs will be read,
No blood of ours conjoined that it might praise
Will sing our legend into further days—
The Chronicler is dead!

Then praise to death, a better host than we,
Housing the heavenly pilgrim for a while.
Though I would substitute for death to see
The immaculate trust of that one boyish smile;
And wait with surety the tread
Of filial feet, and feel myself secure
Against Time's question, honored and obscure—
The Chronicler is dead!

Harold Vinal

NOTATION FROM ELBA

Remember us, exiles by dead water,
Beyond wars and greatness,
Beyond fighting and terror,
Keeping festival with time
Upon this island.

What expectation propelled us
To make this journey, what oracle spoke,
What news was published,
That we should wrest from the sea
This traffic with disaster?

Was it *his* ghost that walked
These murmurous sands,
Hearing the groundswell?

O Trafalgar! Trafalgar!
Where are the armadas?
Where are the battalions?

Remember us, exiles who consider
Hope in this place, who came thence
To drink the wine of a legend,
But left our garlands on an empty altar.

Why are the cannons quiet? We must take
Moscow before the morning.
Josephine, where are you?

It is borne in upon us daily
That this island will profit us nothing;
In these precincts,
Winds are no longer favorable for a return,
Our fortunes are grievous.

Remember us, exiles by dead water,
Beyond wars and greatness,
Beyond fighting and terror,
Keeping festival with time
Upon this island.

O Trafalgar! Trafalgar!
Where are the armadas?
Where are the battalions?

Eleanor Glenn Wallis

SUMMER BARELY HEARD

Plow and pasture lie
    Hot in April sun:
Oats are thrusting high,
    Quail and pipit run
    Quit of dog and gun.

Where a sandy lane
    Skirts a river shallow,
Narrow-shank, the crane
    Wades among the mallow
    Blooms as white as tallow.

Water sucks at rush;
    Hawthorn twigs are spurred;
In the elder bush
    Summer, barely heard,
    Rustles like a bird.

May Williams Ward

MY LITTLE SISTER

My little sister had everything
Everything in the world:
Blue eyes, dimples, pink cheeks,
And her hair curled.

She played forward at basketball
And shot ducks from cover;
She had a sweet rose-colored hat
And a tall lover.

All her life she had everything,
Plenty and more than plenty;
She did not need a perfect death,
Death at twenty.

James E. Warren, Jr.

THE SWAN
(Leamington Spa, England)

In the green gardens stretched by the green river
Almost at noonday had the thin rain slackened,
And briefly where the lone damp benches beckoned
I sat and watched the clouds foam heavily over.

There sharply, clearly on the stony ledge
Of brittle silence carved across the morning
There came, I thought, the tone of hoof-beats. Turning,

I found the street was empty. Still the clatter
Swept eerily on. Then from beneath the bridge
A bright thing burst, where like a snowy hammer
Its wing-tips clanged along the metal water
And turned to iron all the somnolent summer.

Watching the ivory machine veer past,
Sensing a sound like that of circling swords,
I saw like fire that emperor of birds
Curve quickly downward its courageous breast,
Crash the slow water to a silver rain,
And, folding its wings, become a swan again.

BATHER SLEEPING

Across the silken couch of sand
She lies for earth to understand,
The burnished blessing of her youth
Upon her forehead like a hand.

For, since the sun has held her close
And loved her much, she is of those
Lured into gold along their limbs
Where once were ivory and rose.

She sleeps in amber. She is one
With the bright beach she gleams upon,
The strong waves leaning toward her mouth,
The lusty opulence of sun.

And where is magic that may tell
The sweet and fiery dreams that fill
The satin blood, the slumbering bone,
The muscles musically still.

She must not speak. She is remote.
She is a poem summer wrote
And left where aching sand and wind
Might whisper to her lovely throat.

Tessa Sweazy Webb

STORM

On the day of this storm there was no sun,
Or if there was, some strange malignant wing
Eclipsed its brightness, and the hour grew one
With all dark hazard. Swift and menacing,
The whirling sky at the high tide of day
Patterned the twilight. Birds sought friendly eaves,
Even the laughing children left their play
At the shrill tumult of the stricken leaves.

The storm's bewildering breath pommeled the grass
One wild and gusty moment. The fierce wind
Rattled the roof, the fence, the casement glass,
And tore the trees until their boughs were thinned.
While dust suffused the air as with a stain—
Then came the thunder and the sheeted rain.

Winifred Welles

THE TWO TWILIGHTS

Were I to sleep long sleep, and, pensive, waking,
    Look over violet fields, where either dawn,
Immaculately gilt, was coolly breaking,
    Or dusk, a bar of amber, had just gone;
    Then I would wonder, lying there alone,
If it were night just made, or morning making.

And though there were no white cock's crystal crowing,
    Though there should be no star-tongued vesper bell,

But only silence, wavelike, lovely, flowing
  Into the sky's thin, honey-edged dark shell,
  And though I should not move, still I could tell
Whether it were light coming or light going.

John Hall Wheelock

UNISON

There is a secret that the sober mood
Of science misses, it will not be bought
By the contriving mind however shrewd—

Within the cell, within the atom sought,
Within the inner center's whirling rings,
Sits the demonic joy that laughs at thought

And is the face behind the mask of things
And is the measure of the choric dance,
The music of the song creation sings.

Who shall unweave the web of Circumstance,
Or trace the pattern in the fugitive
And shifting tapestry of change and chance?

Or, having learned the pattern, who shall give
The answer then? What answer has been given
Ever, to any man, why man should live!

Not in the flesh, not in the spirit even,
Not in the cunning of the brain that rides
In mastery upon the roads of heaven,

Or charts the rhythm of the starry tides,
The answer and the truth are found, but where,
Deep at the very core, the Stranger bides—

And pours his courage through the heart's despair,
And works his healing in the body's wound,
And sheds his glory through the spirit. There

The answer is, the wisdom shall be found,
Which is the answer of the greening tree,
Which is the wisdom of the fruitful ground—

A wisdom older and more wise than we,
Dumb with a secret difficult to tell,
And inarticulate with mystery,

For, to define it, were a miracle.
Oh, not in the low moments but the great
The exultant rhythm is made audible

That sways the music at the heart of Fate,
To which Time in his passage and return
Moves, and the burdened heavens, with their weight

Of suns and planets, are moving as they burn—
The harmony in which all modes are bent
To the one meaning that they all must learn,

Of many and divergent meanings blent,
Of motions intricate and manifold,
With various voices weaving one consent!

Nor is it easy for the mind to hold
The extreme joy of things, or bear for long
The exalted beauty, hidden from of old,

Whose sure intent, immutable and strong,
Secret and tireless and undeterred,
Moves through the mazes of the winding song—

And whosoever in his heart has heard
That music, all his life shall toil to say
The passion of it. But there is no word—

No words are made for it. There is no way.

Margaret Widdemer

HIGH HOUSE

She built a house to lock out hate
With sharp-carved pride for walls and gate
And hedges of bright flatteries
To break the persecuting breeze;
She heaped up coins of praise and charm
To buy herself from crouching harm
And wove soft cloths of lies and weeping
To blind a spying world to sleeping;
And kept, against a treacherous end,
A needful dagger for each friend.

She had no hope but that last land
Where God, at least, would understand . . .
So, when her waking there befell
Sobbing, she clung to Gabriel:
"Help me, so hunted, hurt and faint!
Never such cross weighed down such saint!
See my scarred lovely hands and side,
One only was so crucified—
Give now my throne of love and praise,
Reward for all my dreadful days!"

But Gabriel's voice fell back from far,
An echo from some unreached star . . .
"How may Love find you to enthrone,
Sealed in your keyless house alone?
Love tried to wake you; but you screamed,
Seeing the demon that you dreamed:
Your own hate forged your own heart's arrow,
Your own sword struck to your own marrow,
Your own hands built this prison-wall. . . .
There was no other foe at all."

Marguerite Wilkinson

NEVER HURT THE PROUD

Never hurt the proud
Lest the wound stay
Long ages through
Like a mark in clay
Till the soul is old,
Till the clay is stone,
And till love is gone.

Speak against the wind,
Or on humble sand
Write the cruel word;
Waves will understand.
Swiftly they will come
To wash the spirit clean
Of mad thought and mean.

Never hurt the proud,
For not every pride
Is so firm in power
That it can deride
Even its own wound.
Oh, let love alone
Be graven on the stone.

B. Y. Williams

OF FOXES

The gray fox for the mountains—
    The gray fox walks alone
In scorn of any comrade
    Save waterfall and stone.
A sparrow for his dinner,
    A cavern for his bed,
The mist-hung world below him,
    A thin moon overhead;
Long hours for meditation
    On mating time and spring,
On hidden oblique pathways
    Or how the planets swing.
Austerity confirms him
    A proper denizen
        For the fastness of the mountains,
            The solitude of mountains.
                And, keeping to the mountains,
    He traffics not with men.

The red fox for the lowlands—
    The red fox has a need
For measuring his cunning,
    For matching speed with speed.
He knows the taste of ducklings
    Made fat by farmers' corn;
He savors the elation
    Of huntsman, hounds and horn.
O splendid hour of testing:
    Outguessing every guess,
Outwitting duller creatures
    With delicate finesse!
And when the chase is ended
    He flaunts his brush again,

A bright torch through the lowlands
To fire the stolid lowlands,
A challenge to the lowlands
For the "view halloo" of men.

George Edward Woodberry

WILD EDEN

There is a garden enclosed
In the high places,
But never hath love reposed
In its bowery spaces;
And the cedars there like shadows
O'er the moonlit champaign stand
Till light like an angel's hand
Touches Wild Eden.

Who told me the name of the garden
That lieth remote, apart,
I know not, nor whence was the music
That sang it into my heart;
But just as the loud robin tosses
His notes from the elm tops high,
As the violets come in the mosses
When south winds wake and sigh,
So on my lips I found it,
This name that is made my cry.

There, under the stars and the dawns
Of the virginal valleys,
White lilies flood the low lawns
And the rose lights the alleys;
But never are heard there the voices
That sweeten on lovers' lips,

And the wild bee never sips
Sweets of Wild Eden.

But who hath shown me the vision
Of the roses and lilies in ranks
I would that I knew, that forever
To him I might render thanks;
For a maiden grows there in her blossom,
In the place of her maidenhood,
Nor knows how her virgin bosom
Is stored with the giving of good,
For the truth is hidden from her
That of love is understood.

No bird with his mate there hovers,
Nor beside her has trilled or sung;
No bird in the dewy covers
Has built a nest for his young;
And over the dark-leaved mountains
The voice in the laurel sleeps;
And the moon broods on the deeps
Shut in Wild Eden.

O Love, if thou in thy hiding
Art he who above me stands,
If thou givest wings to my spirit,
If thou art my heart and my hands—
Through the morn, through the noon, through the even
That burns with thy planet of light,
Through the moonlit space of heaven,
Guide thou my flight
Till, star-like on the dark garden,
I fall in the night!

Fly, song of my bosom, unto it
Wherever the earth breathes spring;
Though a thousand years were to rue it,
Such a heart beats under thy wing,
Thou shalt dive, thou shalt soar, thou shalt find it,

And forever my life be blest,
Such a heart beats in my breast—
Fly to Wild Eden!

Catharine Morris Wright

TRAVELERS IN THE ORIENT

The pikes of Pennsylvania run
Uphill and downhill in the sun,
Bounded by fence and homemade wall,
Familiar and as usual.

The winding Burma Road goes in,
Rocky and singular and thin,
For seven hundred alien miles
Carrying war through its defiles.

Down Plymouth Pike and Old York Road
The seeds of liberty were sowed
By men who marched barefoot and ill
From Germantown and Barren Hill.

Yet from these lanes, still clear with peace,
Americans, for the release
Of everlasting freedom, fly
Pursuit planes in the Burmese sky.

Dissimilar though men may be
They are the same if they are free;
And all their highways run alike;
The Burma Road, the Limekiln Pike.

Frederick A. Wright

LETTER TO THE CITY CLERK

The Honorable the City Clerk: Dear Sir,
I got your notice. In it you refer
To the strange fact that I have not yet paid
My dog license. You say a law was made
That city officers have authority
To kill or sell my dog. Well, let us see.
When Socrates drew one foot on the bed
After his draught of hemlock, Crito said
"What shall we do with you when you have died?"
To that the old philosopher replied
"Crito, you may do anything you please
If you can catch me." Now, like Socrates,
My loving dog, I grieve to say, has gone
Into that spacious mystery where soon
You and all city officers and I
Will follow. Athens doomed her sage to die.
"Nature" he said "has passed the same decree
Upon my judges that they passed on me"
So now you may do anything you please
To my dog if you catch him, except these
Two things that you have threatened, my good sir,
Because it is the special character
Of that state where he is (strange to be told)
That nothing there is ever killed or sold.

Helen M. Wright

SNOW ON AVENUE B

The snow is falling on Avenue B.
Through the school windows the children see
Streets with gutters of ivory.

Coins of silence soon to drown
In the dirty hubbub of the town.
Spendthrift silver whirling down,

Fills the air with windy froth,
Rests on the grime like the wing of a moth
Till the sidewalk is white as an altar cloth.

The tops of the ashcans are covered up
Like a napkin hung on a holy cup,
Filled with ashes for those who sup.

The flakes are drifting star on star,
Made of a cross and a prison bar,
Not more white than the children are.

Margaret Fredericka Wright

WILLOW TREE

What is the green fountain
Softly moving
When the wind is low?
The light behind the onyx mountain,
Slowly fading
As the long days go,

Leaves the tall trees traced with fire,
Dimly burning
Where the prompt stars go
Past roads and trees thrown higher
Than birds flying
In the after glow,

This is the tree of water
Greenly growing
From the dark ground,
Illusion without thought or
Sight or feeling,
A cataract without sound.

Mary J. J. Wrinn

GRECIAN LAMP UNEARTHED NEAR SPARTA

A touch of nature warms this earthen lamp:
Some other woman in the long ago
Poured oil and placed the wax and held it so,
Facing, tight-lipped, Thermopylae's grim camp
As down the wind she caught the ghostly tramp
Of martyred feet. Perhaps its tremulous glow
Caressed the sleeping boy she was to know
Her own one secret hour in the chill damp
Before the Aegean dawn snuffed out the flame.
Night on the heart will light its lamp—the years
Are strewn with wasted wicks of anguish, all
Forgotten at a *heil* to fisted fame.
While through my fingers flow a Spartan's tears,
My sister sets a taper in the hall.

Elinor Wylie

HYMN TO EARTH

Farewell, incomparable element,
Whence man arose, where he shall not return;
And hail, imperfect urn
Of his last ashes, and his firstborn fruit;
Farewell, the long pursuit,
And all the adventures of his discontent;
The voyages which sent
His heart averse from home:
Metal of clay, permit him that he come
To thy slow-burning fire as to a hearth;
Accept him as a particle of earth.

Fire, being divided from the other three,
It lives removed, or secret at the core;
Most subtle of the four,
When air flies not, nor water flows,
It disembodied goes,
Being light, elixir of the first decree,
More volatile than he;
With strength and power to pass
Through space, where never his least atom was:
He has no part in it, save as his eyes
Have drawn its emanation from the skies.

A wingless creature heavier than air,
He is rejected of its quintessence;
Coming and going hence,
In the twin minutes of his birth and death,
He may inhale as breath,
As breath relinquish heaven's atmosphere,
Yet in it have no share,
Nor can survive therein
Where its outer edge is filtered pure and thin:

It doth but lend its crystal to his lungs
For his early crying, and his final songs.

The element of water has denied
Its child; it is no more his element;
It never will relent;
Its silver harvests are more sparsely given
Than the rewards of heaven,
And he shall drink cold comfort at its side:
The water is too wide:
The seamew and the gull
Feather a nest made soft and pitiful
Upon its foam; he has not any part
In the long swell of sorrow at its heart.

Hail and farewell, beloved element,
Whence he departed, and his parent once;
See where thy spirit runs
Which for so long hath had the moon to wife;
Shall this support his life
Until the arches of the waves be bent
And grow shallow and spent?
Wisely it cast him forth
With his dead weight of burdens nothing worth,
Leaving him, for the universal years,
A little seawater to make his tears.

Hail, element of earth, receive thy own,
And cherish, at thy charitable breast,
This man, this mongrel beast:
He ploughs the sand, and, at his hardest need,
He sows himself for seed;
He ploughs the furrow, and in this lies down
Before the corn is grown;
Between the apple bloom
And the ripe apple is sufficient room
In time, and matter, to consume his love
And make him parcel of a cypress grove.

Receive him as thy lover for an hour
Who will not weary, by a longer stay,
The kind embrace of clay;
Even within thine arms he is dispersed
To nothing, as at first;
The air flings downward from its four-quartered tower
Him whom the flames devour;
At the full tide, at the flood,
The sea is mingled with his salty blood:
The traveller dust, although the dust be vile,
Sleeps as thy lover for a little while.

Fay M. Yauger

PLANTER'S CHARM

Slowly Nan the widow goes
Up and down the furrowed rows.

Corn-bags chafing her waist, her hips,
As the kernels fall from her finger-tips:

"One for the buzzard—
One for the crow—
One to rot—and—
One to grow!"

Once she had dreamed (but not of late)
Of another life, of a kinder fate:

Of quiet streets in foreign towns,
Of dancing tunes, and men, and gowns,

But all her dreams were dreamed before
Tim Slade drew rein outside her door.

"One for the buzzard"—Tim was dead
With a bullet hole through his reckless head.

Tim with his cheating ways and words,
Marked from the first for the wart-necked birds.

Tim who had left her sorrowing days,
The farm, and a pair of sons to raise.

Lon was her first-born: "One for the crow!"
Where had he gone? She'd never know

For there was a price upon his head—
"A chip off the old block," people said.

Then "One to rot!" Her thoughts go back,
Like hunting-dogs on an easy track,

To the girl she'd been before she came
To love Tim Slade and bear his name,

And something as stinging and hot as sand
Slides down her cheek and strikes her hand

And she sees the field through a shimmering blur,
For what has marriage meant to her

But a heel of bread in a roofless hut,
Or a crawling course through a mouldy rut?

As if in answer, over the ditch
A child comes riding a willow switch:

Her second-born, of whom no one
Could say in truth, "His father's son."

For his chin is firm, and his mouth is grave,
And the look in his eye is bright and brave.

And she, remembering farm-hand talk:
"You lose three seeds to get one stalk,"

Stands tall and proud and her pale cheeks glow
As she drops a kernel: "One to grow!"

Slowly Nan the widow moves
Up and down the furrowed grooves,

Peace in her heart and a smile on her lips
As the kernels fall from her finger-tips:

> "One for the buzzard—
> One for the crow—
> One to rot—and—
> One to grow!"

I REMEMBER

My father rode a horse
 And carried a gun;
He swapped for a living
 And fought for his fun—
I remember his spurs
 A-gleam in the sun.

My father was always
 Going somewhere—
To rodeo, market,
 Or cattleman's fair—
I remember my mother,
 Her hand in the air.

Marguerite Young

THE FUNERAL

It is late, I said: there will be a cold rain
This eve, and the willow leaves are whitening
And the moon, brighter in shower, as stars divide,
I said, will fall like rain. I said the earth would glide

From its moorings then, and we not know
But be ourselves the convoy to the soul.
And I said the mourners would be amazed then
Muffled in grave cloths of a silver stain

And every mourner would wear a silver crown,
I said, and be to himself the body of death.
And I said earth here would no more be
But butterflies in orbits over the dry sea.

And it all seemed simple, ample, and profound.
The farmer tethered his horse in the tremulous
Evening light, as he had always done
There under the cirrus of the sky's pale green.

But on our eyes there was a driven cloud, a mist,
And earth was turning on another course.
I felt its turn blindfolded as I seemed
And knew no road but what my heart had named,

And knew no road. I heard the neighing wind,
The creak of wheels. And earth was turning on another way,
I felt its turn with funeral, the moon and stars.
So did earth amble outward, cortege or hearse.

VOYAGER MAN

He, voyager man, whom old cosmologies framed
Between the upper and the under air,

He where the winds twelve-blowing as the hours
Struck on his ship with the dull thud of the sea,

There where the waters calmed familiar and kind
He saw the striped dust blown from far inland
The poppy seeds of inland sleep and butterflies
Falling in furrows on the cold, salt wave

And saw how far, the shore of white steaming rock
Whitened by dung of white sea birds, a beach
No tide hurries near but ever outward bears
The sea-bound, early voyager

                              with orange clouds of butterflies
in the loud, loud, loud sea falling
O, with what pollen from the beautiful planet
dust of the regal shore

Earth is the loneliest voyager.

THE RAVEN

And the raven takes but a single wife for life,
A wild lady is yokemate to his flight,
Imperishable lady! in time his greying wife,
They are yoked as oxen in that day's hard light

So late, late is she his soul's greying bride,
For wedded was he to one in a gold epithalamium
And faithful spouse is he to that singular one
When stars like leaves autumnal sigh in time

And if he be widowed, then loneliest will he go
As any cynic bird, who views the viewless waste
And all that emptiness of night and death,
For he is then dour mourner of all moons deceased

And extra-terrestrial raven then is he
Who sees from his vast crags no city of pearl
Where she may dwell, no dove of love to lead
Home, home to him, the raven's transient girl

But the frost-wreathed heath he sees; and it is high funeral
He holds for the empty house of hair and straw
And dirge for fleshly populaces in the wind, and all,
And earth, and a gaping scarecrow vain now.

ACKNOWLEDGMENTS

For permission to include copyrighted material reprinted in this Anthology, grateful acknowledgment is made to the following authors, authors' representatives, and publishers:

D. APPLETON-CENTURY COMPANY, INC. for "Of One Self-Slain" from *Selected Poems* by Charles Hanson Towne and "Old Age" from *Collected Poems* by Cale Young Rice.

A. & C. BONI for "Wild Duck Song" from *Ships and Lovers* by Thomas Caldecot Chubb.

CONTEMPORARY POETRY for "For a Dancer" and "Midnight Eden" from *For the Unlost* by Josephine Jacobsen.

COWARD-McCANN, INC. for "Indian Spring" reprinted from *Songs of the Coast Dwellers* by Constance Lindsay Skinner, copyright 1930 by Coward-McCann, Inc.

JAMES A. DECKER PRESS for "Lost Child" from *Selected Poems* by August Derleth; "Only the Years" from *Only the Years* by Ruth Lechlitner; "It Was Good for the Hebrew Children" from *The Dark Rain Falling* by Gilbert Maxwell; "Summer Barely Heard" from *Tidewater Country* by Eleanor Glenn Wallis.

THE DIAL PRESS for "Locket for the Heart" from *Winter Is a Shadow* by Leila Jones.

DOUBLEDAY & COMPANY, INC. for "Long and Lovely" from *Selected Poems* by Arthur Davison Ficke; "My Mirror" from *Candles That Burn* by Aline Kilmer; and "Prayer of a Soldier in France" from *Poems, Essays and Letters* by Joyce Kilmer.

E. P. DUTTON & COMPANY, INC. for "The One Ambassador" from *My Talon in Your Heart* by Nancy Bruff; "Pierrette in Memory" from *Loves and Losses of Pierrot* by William Griffith; "On the Vanity of Earthly Greatness" from *Gaily the Troubadour* by Arthur Guiterman; "Credo," "Human Throne" and "Under Glass" from *Selected Poems 1912-1944* by Alfred Kreymborg; "Brief Enterprise" and "What Spirit?" from *Brief Enterprise* by Alice Monks Mears; "Knowing What Time It Is at Night" and "Refraction" from *Water and Light* by Louise Townsend Nicholl; and "Whose Eye Is on the Sparrow" from *Ballad of the Bones & Other Poems* by Byron Herbert Reece.

THE FINE EDITIONS PRESS for "Song Comes Like a Frustrated Flower" from *Release the Lark* by John Black; "Farmer's Wife" from *Half the Music* by Bianca Bradbury; "Of Poems" from *Boy at Dusk* by Ralph Friedrich; "Carpentry" from *Mill Talk & Other Poems* by Leslie Nelson Jennings; "Diana Remembers Actaeon" from *Where Stillness Lies the Deepest* by Jessie Lemont; "Two Powers" from *Sight and Sound* by Anne Lloyd; "New York" from *The Invisible Wife & Other Poems* by Winthrop Palmer; and "Weaver" from *Skyways* by Rosa Coates Richards.

HARCOURT, BRACE AND COMPANY, INC. for "Askew, We Ask You," "Behind Dark Spaces" and "Hymn to Night" from *Poems, New and Selected* by Melville Cane, copyright 1938 by Melville Cane. By permission of Harcourt, Brace and Company, Inc.

HARPER & BROTHERS for "Grecian Lamp" and "Unearthed Near Sparta" from *Cock on the Ridge* by Mary J. J. Wrinn and "Dust" from *The Closed Gentian* by Elizabeth Hollister Frost.

HENRY HOLT & COMPANY for "The Mind Has Studied Flight" and "Awake Under Stars" from *Natural History* by Raymond Holden; "To a Wild Goose Over Decoys," "Four Little Foxes" and "Cattle Bells" from *Collected Poems* by Lew Sarett; and "A Considerable Speck," "Come In" and "The Most of It" from *A Witness Tree* by Robert Frost.

HOUGHTON MIFFLIN COMPANY for "In the Beginning Was the Word" from *A Lock Box & Other Poems* by Anna Hempstead Branch; "Cradle Song" from *Collected Poems* by Josephine Preston Peabody; "The Hawthorn" from *The Moving Tide* by Jessie B. Rittenhouse; and "Wild Eden" from *Selected Poems* by George Edward Woodberry.

BRUCE HUMPHRIES, INC. for "Morning without Malice" from *The Dark Gaze* by Elda Tanasso.

KALEIDOGRAPH PRESS for "I Am Desert-Born" from *Locoed & Other Poems* by Vaida S. Montgomery.

MITCHELL KENNERLEY for "Stains" from *The Joy o' Life* by Theodosia Garrison.

ALFRED A. KNOPF, INC. for "Love" from *The Forerunner* by Kahlil Gibran; "Child on the Beach" from *This, My Letter* by Sara Henderson Hay; "The Grass" from *Red Drumming in the Sun* by May Lewis; "Pieties" from *Poems 1920-1945* by David Morton; "Tasting the Earth" from *The Sea* by James Oppenheim; "Confidants" from *Collected Poems* by William Alexander Percy; "Most Sacred Mountain" from *Profiles from China* by Eunice Tietjens; and "Hymn to Earth" from *Collected Poems* by Elinor Wylie.

THE LEAGUE TO SUPPORT POETRY for "Apology to My Heirs" from *There Is Still Time* by Carolyn Wilson Link.

LIVERIGHT PUBLISHING CORPORATION for "Sitting-Room in a Bowery Hotel" from *Man in the Shadows* by Elias Lieberman.

THE MACMILLAN COMPANY for "The Secret Heart" from *Collected Poems* by Robert P. Tristram Coffin; "The Crowning Gift" from *Poems* by Gladys Cromwell; "Doors" from *Poems and Ballads* by Hermann Hagedorn; "Abraham Lincoln Walks at Midnight" from *Collected Poems* by Vachel Lindsay; "My Love and I" from *My Lady Dear, Arise!* by Percy MacKaye; "Riddles 1, 2 and 3" from *Selected Poems* by Sister M. Madeleva; "The Water Ouzel" from *Chosen Poems* by Harriet Monroe; "Flammonde" from *Collected Poems* by Edwin Arlington Robinson; "As I Came Down Lebanon" from *The Singing Heart* by Clinton Scollard; "Man Is Forever Lonely" from *Ritual For Myself* by Anderson M. Scruggs; "Arcturus in Autumn" from *Collected Poems* by Sara Teasdale; "Harvest Home," "Prothalamium," and "Three O'Clock" from *Poems 1941* by Ridgely Torrence; and "Never Hurt the Proud" from *Citadels* by Marguerite Wilkinson.

NEW DIRECTIONS for "Wild Apples" from *And You, Thoreau* by August Derleth.

PANTHEON BOOKS, INC. for "Flight into Darkness" and "On the Struma Massacre" from *Flight into Darkness* by Ralph Gustafson.

G. P. PUTNAM'S SONS for "And the Days Were Accomplished" from *No Special Pleading* by Mary Ballard Duryee; "Oxen" from *Quarried Crystals* by Mary Cummings Eudy; "He Who Loves the Ocean" from *Spider Architect* by Mary Sinton Leitch; and "Bargain" from *Strange Dimension* by Florence Dickinson Stearns.

REYNAL AND HITCHCOCK, INC. for "The Funeral," "The Raven" and "Voyager Man" from *Moderate Fable* by Marguerite Young.

RINEHART & COMPANY, INC. for "American Names" from *Ballads and Poems: 1915-1930* by Stephen Vincent Benét; "The Mountain Woman" from *Jasbo Brown & Selected Poems* by DuBose Heyward; and "Clonmacnoise" from *Shadow of the Perfect Rose* by Thomas S. Jones, Jr.

CHARLES SCRIBNER'S SONS for "Encounter" from *Selected Poems* by John Peale Bishop; "We Are Wonderful, We Are Wise" from *War Songs* by Struthers Burt; "O World" from *Poems* by George Santayana; and "Unison" from *Poems 1911-1936* by John Hall Wheelock.

ALAN SWALLOW for "Mortal Hunger" and "Golden Leopard" from *Mortal Hunger* by Gustav Davidson.

TALARIA PUBLICATIONS for "Of Foxes" from *Far Is the Hill* by B. Y. Williams.

THE VIKING PRESS, INC. for "Address to the Doomed, I, II, IX" from *The Flowering Stone* by George Dillon; "Sonnets" from *Two Lives* by William Ellery Leonard; and "The Two Twilights" from *Blossoming Antlers* by Winifred Welles.

THE WINGS PRESS for "The Woods Shall Not Be Lonely" from *Green Vistas* by Stanton A. Coblentz.

YALE UNIVERSITY PRESS for "I Shall Be Loved as Quiet Things" from *Burning Bush* by Karle Wilson Baker.

ACCENT for "Concept" by Gertrude May Lutz.

AMERICA for "Crowning" by Laura Benét and "Tropical Fish" by Gertrude Ryder Bennett.

AMERICAN MERCURY for "Siesta Hour" by Clifford Gessler; "End of Farce" by James Rorty; and "Invocation" by Sydney King Russell.

ATLANTIC MONTHLY for "Trammeled Swimmer" by William Rose Benét; Days at Sea" by May Lewis; "Elegy under the Stars" by Anne Morrow Lindbergh; "At the Shore" by Edwin Morgan, and "Freedom Considered" by Harriet Sampson.

BRITAIN for "Apostrophe to a Fighter Plane" by Virginia T. McCormick.

CHRISTIAN CENTURY for "Cathedral" by Sara King Carleton.

CIRCLE MAGAZINE for "Translation from a Lost Language" by Minna Gellert.

COMMON SENSE for "A Memorial for Mr. Jefferson" by Coleman Rosenberger.

COMMONWEAL for "Bagpipes" by Shaemas O'Sheel and "Harper's Ferry" by Carl John Bostelmann.

CHRISTIAN SCIENCE MONITOR for "Tracks" by Elizabeth Bohm; "Blue Heron" by Yetza Gillespie; "Weaver" by Rosa Coates Richards; and "New Hampshire" by Rosemary Thomas.

CONTEMPORARY POETRY for "Foundation" by Frances Minturn Howard.

EVENING BULLETIN (Philadelphia) for "Travelers in the Orient" by Catharine Morris Wright.

FLORIDA MAGAZINE OF VERSE for "Strawberry Mark" by Florence Kerr Brownell and "Black Soldier" by Elizabeth J. Buchtenkirk.

HARPER'S MAGAZINE for "Small Apocalypse" by Earl Daniels and "New Wonder" by John Williams Andrews.

KALEIDOGRAPH for "Epitaph: Written in Snow" by Jessie Wilmore Murton and "The Swan" by James E. Warren, Jr.

LANTERN for "Le Printemps Empoissonné" by Frances W. Butterfield.

LYRIC for "Instant out of Time" by Amanda B. Hall and "April's Daughter" by Virginia L. Tunstall.

NATION for "Ophidia" by Gwendolen Haste.

NATURAL HISTORY MAGAZINE for "Two Deer in a Glade" by Helen Morrow.

NEW MASSES for "When Bombs on Barcelona Burst" by Louis Ginsberg.

NEW REPUBLIC for "Defeat" by Witter Bynner and "Death of the Grandmother" by Gwendolen Haste.

NEW YORK HERALD TRIBUNE for "Prevision" by Ruth Lambert Jones and "Counsel for Youth" by A. M. Sullivan.

NEW YORK TIMES for "When a Gull Falls" by Holger Lundbergh.

NEW YORKER for "The Zoo in the City" by Sara Van Alstyne Allen and "David Today" by Alexander Laing, copyright The F-R. Publishing Corporation, by courtesy of the New Yorker in which these poems originally appeared.

POETRY: A MAGAZINE OF VERSE for "House Long Known" by Amy Bonner; "Short Story" by Henry Dalton; "Children on a Hill" by Marion Ethel Hamilton; "The Hand" by Dorothy Berry Hughes; "The Deaf" by

Gordden Link; "Drought" by Edith Mirick; "Phoenix" by Grace Fallow Norton; "The Weeper" by Leonora Speyer; "My Little Sister" by May Williams Ward; "Bather Sleeping" by James E. Warren, Jr.; and "Storm" by Tessa Sweazy Webb.

POETRY CHAP-BOOK for "The Magnolia Tree" by Marjorie Meeker; "Elegy for a Lost Continent" by Margaret R. Richter; "Fit Remembrance" by I. L. Salomon; and "Prayer in an Arctic Season" by Marguerite J. Adams.

PRAIRIE SCHOONER for "The Dark Chamber" by Ethel Romig Fuller.

SATURDAY REVIEW OF LITERATURE for "Portrait of Two Unhappy Young People" by Dorothy Alyea; "Late Summer" by William Rose Benét; "Eight Doves" by Jane Dransfield; "Martyr" by Frances M. Howard; "Low Country" by Josephine Johnson; "Museum Piece" by Gordon Lawrence; "To My Brothers Everywhere" by Elias Lieberman; "Camouflage of the Willow Ptarmigan" by Mary Owings Miller; "Mouse in a Florist's Window" by Virginia Scott Miner; "The Skeleton on the Shore" by Starr Nelson; "In Space The One Great Ornament" by Louise Townsend Nicholl; "Broadcast to the Scholars in the Eyrie" by David Ross; "These Poems I Have So Loved" and "Note to 'Fiddler's Farewell' " by Leonora Speyer.

SPIRIT for "Winter Overture" by Lucy Kent; "November Afternoons" by Sister M. Madeleva; "There is a Street" by Gerard Previn Meyer; "Coronal" by Ruth Forbes Sherry; and "The Chronometer" by A. M. Sullivan.

VERSECRAFT for "Sleep" by Sophie Himmell.

VIRGINIA QUARTERLY REVIEW for "The Quick Still Center" by Elizabeth Randall-Mills.

VOICES for "The Great Square" by Jane Dransfield; "The Cocks Have Crowed" by Rosemary Farrar; "The Aristocrat" and "Signature Upon Rock" by Elizabeth Stanton Hardy; "Awakening" by Dorothy Hobson; "Harvest" by Mary Hoxie Jones; "Wandering Child" by Fania Kruger; "The Grass" by May Lewis; "Skunk Cabbage Rising in March" by Sarah Litsey; "Rococo Summer" by Lawrence Perry Spingarn; "From An Ivory Tower" by Helen Frith Stickney; and "Sun Through Window Shutters" by Anne Sotherne Tardy.

WASHINGTON POST for "The Stallion" by Elma Dean; "Golgotha" by Gertrude M. Lutz; "The Little Progress" by Mary Atwater Taylor; and "The School Boy Learns to Fly" by Amanda Benjamin Hall.

WASHINGTON STAR for "Emily Dickinson" by Mae Winkler Goodman.

YALE REVIEW for "A Star by Day" by David McCord.

———

ESTELLE DUCLO for "O Nations!"

MRS. THEODORE DREISER for "Evening-Mountains" by Theodore Dreiser.

ORRICK JOHNS for "Tree Toad" and "Wild Plum."

VIRGIL MARKHAM for "Lincoln, The Man of the People" by Edwin Markham.

BIOGRAPHICAL NOTES

ADAMS, MARGUERITE JANVRIN is the author of two collections of poems, *I Give You Words* (Ives, Washburn 1935) and *Insignia Amoris* (The Fine Editions Press 1940), and is a frequent contributor of verse to magazines and newspapers. She is a New Yorker by birth and residence.

ALLEN, SARA VAN ALSTYNE was born in Philadelphia. She is a graduate of Pomona College (Cal.). Her work has appeared in many periodicals, including the New Yorker, Saturday Review of Literature, Poetry, Yale Review, etc.

ALYEA, DOROTHY is an alumna of Wellesley. A native of Portland, Ore., she makes her home in Montclair, N. J. She has published one volume of verse, *All My Argument* (1935).

ANDREWS, JOHN WILLIAMS received his A.B. degree from Yale in 1920 and was International News Service correspondent and manager of the Chung-Mei News Agency, in Peking, China in 1921-22. He received his L.L.B. degree from Yale in 1926. After practicing law in New York he became a free lance writer, publishing *Prelude to 'Icaros'* (Farrar & Rinehart 1936), and other books and poems, including *History of the Founding of Wolf's Head* (1934), *Georgia Transport* (Columbia Work Shop 1937), *A Ballad of Channel Crossings* (Timothy Dwight College Press, 1942), etc. He has contributed verse to Harpers, Yale Review, Saturday Review of Literature, etc. He is Chief of the Federal-State Relations Section of the Department of Justice, Washington, D. C. He is a native of New Haven, Conn.

AUSTIN, MARY (1868-1934) moved, at the age of eighteen, from the midwest to the California desert where she remained for sixteen years, studying primitive Indian life. She took up a writing profession after the death of her child. Establishing a home in Santa Fé, she produced more than a score of books, including valuable translations and dramas based on Indian and Spanish folk lore. Her autobiography, *Earth Horizon,* appeared in 1932.

BAKER, KARLE WILSON of Nacogdoches, Tex. is a native of Little Rock, Ark. She holds an honorary Litt.D. degree from Southern Methodist University. Among her nine published volumes are two works of fiction and three collections of verse. Her first book in the latter field was *Blue Smoke* (1919) followed by *Burning Bush* (1922), both brought out by the Yale University Press.

BARKER, ELSA was born in Leicester, Vt. and makes her home in New York City. Her published works include three books of verse: *The Frozen Grail & Other Poems* (Duffield 1910), *The Book of Love*

(Duffield 1912) and *Songs of a Vagrom Angel* (Kennerley 1916), and nine prose volumes, among them *The Son of Mary Bethel, Letters from a Living Dead Man,* and *Fielding Sargent.* In 1942 she won the Lola Ridge award with her poem The Iron Age. She is a charter member of the PSA.

BARR, ISABEL HARRISS is a graduate of the College of New Rochelle with the degree of B. Litt. cum laude. A native of Greenville, Tex., she makes her home in Larchmont, N. Y. Her *Sword Against the Breast,* a volume of poems, was published by Putnam in 1935. She is also the author of *In the Beginning,* a trilogy of one-act plays (Walter Baker 1945).

BENET, LAURA is a Vassar graduate. Early in life she engaged in social settlement work, following that with editorial writing on newspapers. In World War II she was active as a Red Cross Gray Lady. Member of a distinguished writing family (Stephen Vincent and William Rose Benét are her brothers), she is the author of eleven volumes of poetry and prose, including a novelized biography of Emily Dickinson entitled *Come Slowly, Eden* (Dodd, Mead 1942). Her most recent published work is *Washington Irving: Explorer of American Legend* (1944). She lives in New York City and is on the executive board of the PSA.

BENET, STEPHEN VINCENT (1898-1943) was born in Bethlehem, Pa. When he entered Yale at the age of seventeen he had already published his first book of poems, *Five Men and Pompey.* He was still an undergraduate when his *Young Adventure* was published by Yale University Press; and his third volume of poems, *Heaven and Earth,* served as his M.A. thesis. While living in France he worked on the long narrative poem *John Brown's Body,* which won him the Pulitzer award in 1929. His published work includes subsequent collections of poetry, novels, short stories, and radio dramas. His Book I of an uncompleted American epic, *Western Star,* was published posthumously and awarded the Pulitzer prize for poetry in 1944. Commenting on this final work, Henry Seidel Canby said of its author: "He is perhaps the first of the poets prophesied by Whitman."

BENET, WILLIAM ROSE was born at Fort Hamilton, N. Y. Harbor, of an Army family. He was graduated from the Albany Academy and the Sheffield Scientific School and holds honorary M.A. and Litt.D. degrees from Yale University and Dickinson College. Since the appearance in 1913 of his first book of poems, *Merchants From Cathay,* he has written, edited and published more than twenty-three volumes in poetry and prose. His semi-autobiographical novel in verse *The Dust Which Is God* received the Pulitzer prize in 1942 and was reissued by Knopf in 1945. His most recent book of poems, *Day of Deliverance,* appeared in 1944. Among the volumes he has edited are *The Oxford Anthology of American Literature* (in collaboration with Norman Holmes Pearson) and the recent Modern Library *Anthology of Famous English and American Poetry* (with Conrad Aiken). He is a vice-president of the National Institute of Arts and Letters and a vice-president of the PSA. He has been on the staff of The Saturday Review of Literature since that magazine's inception in 1923.

BENNETT, GERTRUDE RYDER lives in Brooklyn, the borough of her birth. She holds B.S. and M.A. degrees from New York University and Columbia. She is the author of *Etched in Words* (Putnam 1938).

BISHOP, JOHN PEALE (1892-1944), a West Virginian by birth, was graduated from Princeton in 1917 and went overseas in World War I as a first lieutenant in the infantry. Following an interval as managing editor of Vanity Fair, he made his home in France for over a decade. On his return to the United States he was made a fellow of the Library of Congress and served as Special Consultant at the Office of Coordinator of Inter-American Affairs. With Allen Tate he edited *Twenty Years of Creative Writing in the United States*. His published work includes *The Undertaker's Garland* (with Edmund Wilson), his *Selected Poems* (1941) and other collections of poetry and prose.

BLACK, JOHN came to this country from Scotland at the age of twelve. At twenty-two he was literary editor of the Brooklyn Daily Eagle. Subsequently he held the posts of associate editor of McClure's and Current History. On his return from overseas in World War I, he founded the first Joyce Kilmer Post and was elected National President of the American Legion Founders. He is co-editor of *Gathering of the Forces,* a collection of Whitman writings, and is the author of three books of verse, the latest, *Release the Lark,* issued in 1946 by The Fine Editions Press.

BOHM, ELIZABETH (Mrs. Hugo Schwarz) was born in London, the daughter of the noted artist, Max Bohm. Her education she describes as "sketchy". A frequent contributor of poetry to leading journals, she has won many prizes at the monthly gatherings of the PSA. She makes her home in New York City.

BONNER, AMY is a native and resident of New York City. Since 1937 she has been Eastern Representative of Poetry: A Magazine of Verse, where her work has frequently appeared. She has served on the New York Evening Post as an editor, columnist and editorial writer, and as poetry critic for that newspaper as well as for the New York World-Telegram, Christian Science Monitor and Brooklyn Daily Eagle. Her articles have appeared in many national publications. She conducted the poetry symposiums at the Brooklyn Institute of Arts and Sciences. She is a member of the executive board of the PSA and chairman of its Poets' Fund.

BOSTELMANN, CARL JOHN is an industrial advertising executive by profession. He was born in Lyndhurst, N. J. and received his education at the Rutherford High School. His published works include *April Comes Early* (Harold Vinal 1928), *Neighbor John* (Stackpole Sons 1936), and *Songs from Shelley* and *Track and Field,* both published by the Colonial Press in 1937.

BRADBURY, BIANCA of Mystic, Conn. received her B.A. from the Connecticut College for Women in 1930. Her work has appeared in many anthologies, magazines and newspapers. *Half the Music,* her first book of poems, was published by The Fine Editions Press in 1944. She is author of several books for children, the latest in this field being *The Antique Cat* (Winston 1945).

BRADSHAW, ANN, a native of Lamar, Mo., moved to Washington, D. C. during the late war and served as recording secretary of the Woman's National Democratic Club. She studied verse technique under Jessica Nelson North and attended Columbia University. She has a volume of poetry under way.

BRANCH, ANNA HEMPSTEAD (1875-1937) was born in New London, Conn., graduated from Smith College in 1897 and moved to New York to devote the greater part of her life to social service. Christadora House was a special project of hers. Some of our finest mystic poetry is to be found in her work, which includes *Nimrod,* a 2,000 line poem. *The Last Poems of Anna Hempstead Branch,* edited by Ridgely Torrence, appeared in 1944 under the Farrar & Rinehart imprint. She was a charter member of the PSA.

BROWNELL, FLORENCE KERR is a native of Buffalo, N. Y. She spends her winters in California, her summers in Maine. A special student at Boston University and Columbia in short story technique, she prefers writing poetry. Her work appears frequently in the current magazines.

BRUFF, NANCY (Mrs. E. T. Clarke) was born in Fairfield, Conn. of pioneer stock. She was educated in various schools in her native state and at the Sorbonne in Paris. She is the author of a recent, best-selling novel, *The Manatee,* and of a first book of verse, *My Talon in Your Heart* (1946), both published by Dutton.

BUCHTENKIRK, ELIZABETH J. is a graduate of Bradford Junior College (Mass.). She spent her early married life in France, where her two daughters were born. Her poems appear in various periodicals. She is a native of Orange, N. J.

BURLIN, HELEN divides her time between New York City and Woodstock, N. Y. A native of Boston, she received her education in that city and in Paris. She first pursued a musical career and has published one collection of poems *In the Midst of Death* (Harbinger House 1944). Her translation of a section of Aragon's prose appears in *Aragon: Poet of the French Resistance* (Duell, Sloan & Pearce 1945).

BURT, STRUTHERS studied at Princeton and at Oxford, and was a reporter on the Philadelphia Times. Since 1908 he has been a Wyoming rancher. He is the author of many volumes of verse, fiction, and critical prose, including *The Diary of a Dude Wrangler, The Delectable Mountains, Along These Streets,* etc. His latest book, *Philadelphia: Holy Experiment,* appeared in 1945 (Doubleday & Co.). He was born in Baltimore.

BURTON, RICHARD (1861-1940) was a poet in the Yankee tradition. His first book of verse, *Dumb in June,* appeared in 1895. In 1931, when he was seventy, his seven published collections of poetry were edited and reissued in one volume as *The Collected Poems of Richard Burton* with an introduction by Alfred Kreymborg. He was a charter member of the PSA.

BUTTERFIELD, FRANCES WESTGATE was born in Norfield, Miss. She received her B.A. from Randolph-Macon Woman's College and her M.A. from Columbia University. In 1943 she enlisted in the WAC and in 1944 was commissioned a Second Lieutenant. She is the author of poems and articles published in this country and abroad. She now writes publicity for the Board of Education in New York.

BYNNER, WITTER, now a resident of New Mexico, was born in Brooklyn. After graduating from Harvard he traveled extensively, chiefly in the Orient. His *The Jade Mountain* (1929) was the earliest comprehensive collection of Chinese poetry to be translated into English by an American poet. He published eighteen volumes in poetry and drama. His latest book, an "American version" of *The Way of Life According to Laotzu,* appeared in 1944 (John Day). The most recent collection of his own poems, *Against the Cold,* was issued in 1940. He is a charter member of the PSA, and a past president (1920-22).

CANE, MELVILLE, a resident New Yorker and an attorney by profession, hails from Plattsburg, N. Y. He received his A.B. (1900) and LL.B. (1903) from Columbia University. The most recent of his three volumes of verse is *Poems, New and Selected* (Harcourt, Brace 1938). He contributes poems and articles, both serious and satirical, to The Saturday Review of Literature, The New Yorker, Prairie Schooner, etc.

CARLETON, SARA KING, of Sharon, Conn. and New York City, is the author of one book of verse, *To All Wayfarers,* brought out in 1940 by The Fine Editions Press. Her work has appeared in The Commonweal, Harper's, The Christian Century, New York Times, Poetry Chap-Book, etc.

CARMAN, BLISS (1861-1929) was born in Canada. He issued his first book of lyrics, *Low Tide on Grand Pré,* soon after taking up residence in the United States. His *Songs From Vagabondia,* written in collaboration with Richard Hovey, established his fame. He published more than twenty volumes of essays and poems, the best of them in his well-known "vagabond" vein. He was a charter member of the PSA.

CAWEIN, MADISON (1865-1914), called at one time "The Keats of Kentucky," spent most of his life in his native state. He was the author of twenty volumes of poetry, produced during the nineteen years of his employment as cashier in a Kentucky gambling house. He was a charter member of the PSA.

CHAPIN, KATHERINE GARRISON (Mrs. Francis Biddle) was born in Waterford, Conn. She is the author of five volumes of poetry. Her *Plain-Chant for America* was a Harper publication for 1942. Previous titles include *Outside of the World* (1930) and *Bright Mariner* (1933), both brought out by Duffield, and *Time Has No Shadow* (Dodd, Mead 1936).

CHUBB, THOMAS CALDECOT is a graduate of Yale, where he won the John Masefield prize in poetry. His interest in the Italian Renaissance resulted in two major works in biography: *The Life of Giovanni Boccaccio* and *Aretino, Scourge of Princes*. In the field of poetry he is represented with five books, the most recent, *A Time to Speak,* issued in 1943 by The Fine Editions Press. He is a book reviewer for the New York Times. A life of Achille Murat is in preparation. He was born in East Orange, N. J. and makes his home in Greenwich, Conn.

CLAYTOR, GERTRUDE, native of Staunton, Va. and now resident in New York City, was educated at Virginia College. She is the winner of the PSA first prize for 1933, and composed the poem inscribed on the bronze plaque set up on Skyline Drive, commemorating Governor Spotswood.

COBLENTZ, CATHERINE CATE is an alumna of George Washington University. She hails from Hardwick, Vt. and resides in Washington, D. C. Her fifth book, *The Bells of Leyden Sing* (Longmans, Green), appeared in 1944. Earlier works of hers were brought out by the Atlantic Monthly Press.

COBLENTZ, STANTON A. is a Californian by birth and residence. His principal published works include *The Pageant of Man, Green Vistas, Marching Men, The Decline of Man,* and *When the Birds Fly South.* Recently he edited *The Music Makers,* an anthology of contemporary lyric poetry (Bernard Ackerman 1945). He is the editor and founder of Wings, A Quarterly of Verse.

COFFIN, ROBERT P. TRISTRAM is a native down-Easterner who grew up on a salt-water farm a "stone's throw" from Bowdoin College (Maine) where he is now professor of English. He was graduated from Bowdoin summa cum laude and was a Rhodes Scholar at Oxford. He is the recipient of many honorary degrees. In 1936 he won the Pulitzer prize for poetry with his volume *Strange Holiness.* He wrote the first in the Rivers of America series, *The Kennebec.* His *Collected Poems* appeared in 1939.

CROMWELL, GLADYS (1885-1919) with her twin sister Dorothea went overseas in the Red Cross Canteen Service during World War I. On the way back to America the two girls, in what appeared to be a suicide pact, jumped overboard. The French government conferred on them the Croix de Guerre, posthumously. The best of Gladys' work is contained in her *Poems,* published after her death and awarded the PSA prize in 1920.

DALTON, HENRY was educated at Union University in Jackson, Tenn. and at the University of Virginia. His work has appeared in Poetry, Tomorrow, the Lyric, New York Times, Voices, etc. He was born in Rienzi, Miss.

DANIELS, EARL, born in Millis, Mass., holds degrees from Clark University, the University of Chicago, and Harvard (B.A., M.A., Ph.D.). He is professor of English Literature at Colgate, contributes to various literary journals, and is the author of *The Art of Reading Poetry* (Farrar & Rinehart 1941).

DAVIDSON, GUSTAV came to the United States from Warsaw, Poland, at the age of two. At seventeen he interrupted his studies to visit Palestine where he wrote a poetic play. On his return, after receiving his B.A. and M.A. from Columbia, he entered the field of journalism and served, at various times, as associate editor of the Mirror (N. Y.), editorial writer for the Washington (D. C.) Post, and research bibliographer at the Library of Congress. He helped to launch four poetry magazines. In 1940 he established The Fine Editions Press. He is the author of more than a dozen books in prose, verse and drama. He is a member of the executive board of the PSA.

DAVIES, MARY CAROLYN of New York is the author of works in drama, fiction and poetry. Her first book of poems *The Drums in Our Street* (1918) was followed a year later by *Youth Riding*, both published by Macmillan. *Marriage Songs* (1923), *The Skyline Trail* (1924) and *Penny Show* (1927) are other titles of her work in poetry. She was the first woman undergraduate to win the Emily Chamberlain Cook prize for poetry at the University of California. She was born near Spokane, Wash. and educated in schools in British Columbia, the University of California and New York University.

DAVIS, JULIA JOHNSON hails from Norfolk, Va. She attended Harvard and Columbia and is the author of two books, *Print o' Life* (1930) and *Gribble's, A Beloved Penny Shop* (1932).

DEAN, ELMA was born in Beaver Falls, Pa. and is a resident of Oakland, Cal. She is the winner of several PSA awards. Her work has appeared in the American Mercury, Reader's Digest, The Woman, etc.

DERLETH, AUGUST, one of the most prolific of living writers, is the author of more than two score books in a variety of fields. He is active as poet, historian, editor, book reviewer, and directing head of his own publishing firm, Arkham House. He received a Guggenheim Fellowship in 1938 to encourage further work on his monumental Sac Prairie saga. Decker brought out his *Selected Poems* in 1944. He is a native and resident of Sauk City, Wis.

DE WITT, SAMUEL is a native New Yorker and was educated at the College of the City of New York and New York University Law School. He served in the legislative assembly of New York state as Socialist member. He has published eight volumes of verse and three plays. Among his works in poetry are *Riding the Storm* (1920), *Iron Monger* (1922), *Harvest* (1937), and *More Sonnets to a Dark Lady* (1940). His translation from the German of Walter Mehring's *No Road Back* appeared in 1944. He sponsors the Lola Ridge Memorial Award in the interest of poetry of social significance.

DILLON, GEORGE was born in Jacksonville, Fla. He received a Ph.B. from the University of Chicago, and did graduate work at the University of Paris. His home is in Richmond, Va. His second volume of poems, *Flowerng Stone,* won the Pulitzer prize for poetry in 1932. He was a Guggenheim Fellow in 1932-33. Until World War II intervened he served as editor of Poetry: A Magazine of Verse. His most recent literary work is a translation, with Edna St. Vincent Millay, of Beaudelaire's *Flowers of Evil.*

DOWLING, ALLAN D. is the author of *Truth and Music,* privately printed (1924), *The Kingdom of Towers* (Harold Vinal 1928) and *A Poet's Youth* (The Wanderer Press, 1944). He is a native of New York City.

DRANSFIELD, JANE was born in Rochester, N. Y. and educated at Vassar. She resides in Brooklyn Heights. Her plays, prose and verse have been widely performed in the United States and England. She is the author of *Marks Upon a Stone,* a collection of sonnets and lyrics, published in 1940, and is the winner of a PSA annual award.

DREISER, THEODORE (1871-1945) has been called by many critics the greatest American writer of the 20th century. He was the author of a series of notable—and often controversial—works in fiction but was little known as a poet. His only book in that medium was published by Simon & Schuster in 1935 under the title *Moods, Philosophic and Emotional.* He was born in Terre Haute, Ind. and died at his estate in Mount Kisco, N. Y.

DUCLO, ESTELLE was educated in private schools in this country and in Europe, and majored in languages and comparative literature. She was an active member of the Committee on Literature for the MacDowell Club and conducted many symposia. She is a resident of Brooklyn, N. Y.

DURYEE, MARY BALLARD (Mrs. Samuel Sloan Duryee) contributes to numerous publications. She is the author of three volumes of poetry: *Avenues of Song* (Brick Row Book Shop 1926), *No Special Pleading* (Putnam 1940) and *Free Enterprise* (The Fine Editions Press 1943). She is a native of Philadelphia and served for four years as president of the Women's City Club of New York.

EUDY, MARY CUMMINGS was born in Louisville, Ky. and is now a resident of Winter Park, Fla. She is the author of *Quarried Crystals & Other Poems* published by Putnam in 1935.

FARRAR, ROSEMARY is a Bostonian, now living in Great Barrington, Mass. Her poems have appeared in many leading magazines.

FICKE, ARTHUR DAVISON (1883-1945) was born in Davenport, Iowa. A graduate of Harvard, he taught English and studied law at the University of Iowa through 1907. In that year he turned to poetry. His published works include *Sonnets of a Portrait Painter, The Man on the Hilltop,* and his last volume, *Tumultuous Shore* (Knopf 1942).

He was the author also of a novel, *Mrs. Morton of Mexico.* In 1918, with Witter Bynner, he founded the school of "spectrist poetry."

FISHER, MAHLON LEONARD is a native of Williamsport, Pa. He studied architecture and was for many years a practicing architect. In 1917 he founded, and for a time edited,' The Sonnet. He has published three volumes of poetry and a frequently perfomed choral work, *White Silence.*

FLACCUS, KIMBALL was an instructor at the College of the City of New York before he entered the navy as a lieutenant (in World War II). In 1934 Scribner's published his first book of poems, *Avalanche of April;* in 1940 his second volume *The White Stranger* appeared, also under the Scribner imprint.

FLETCHER, JOHN GOULD is a native and resident of Little Rock, Ark. He attended Harvard and the University of Arkansas (LL.D.) and has traveled extensively abroad. He is the author of a score of volumes in poetry and prose. *Life Is My Song,* an autobiography, appeared in 1937. In 1939 he was awarded the Pulitzer prize for his *Selected Poems.* In 1941 his *South Star* appeared. In the Summer of 1946 Dutton's published his *The Burning Mountain.*

FRIEDRICH, RALPH taught English at Withrow High School in Cincinnati, O. for many years prior to joining the army on a special language assignment. He has had one book of poems published, *Boy at Dusk* (The Fine Editions Press 1942).

FROST, ELIZABETH HOLLISTER of Rochester, N. Y., is the author of three volumes of poems, all under the Harper imprint: *The Lost Lyrist* (1928), *Hovering Shadow* (1929) and *The Closed Gentian* (1931), and two novels published by Coward-McCann.

FROST, ROBERT is commonly regarded as America's foremost living poet. He was born in San Francisco but came East at an early age. He put in brief appearances at Dartmouth and Harvard. For a time he earned a scant living as a school teacher and farmer. His first book of poems, *A Boy's Will,* was published while he was in England (1912-1915). With the publication, in America, of his *North of Boston,* he became famous. By then he was past forty. In 1924, 1937, 1942 and again in 1943 he was awarded the Pulitzer prize for poetry, the only poet to be thus honored four times. He succeeded Edwin Markham as Honorary President of the PSA.

FULLER, ETHEL ROMIG, born in Big Rapids, Mich., has edited for the past fourteen years a widely-known column of verse in The Oregonian. Two collections of her own work have been published, the latest, *Kitchen Sonnets,* by Binsford & Mort in 1931, reprinted in 1938.

GARRISON, THEODOSIA (1874-1919), a native of Newark, N. J., published her first book of poems, *The Joy o' Life,* in 1909. She wrote a great deal of distinctive magazine verse. Her major life interest was in child labor reform, and her *Ballad of the Unbidden Guest* was composed for the Child Labor Committee. She was a charter member of the PSA.

GELLERT, MINNA is a native of New York City. Her work has appeared in Sewanee Review, Contemporary Poetry, Poetry Chap-Book and elsewhere. A group of her poems was included in *New Poets*, published by Decker in 1941.

GESSLER, CLIFFORD is at present a member of the editorial staff of the Oakland Tribune (Cal.). He studied at Milton College and the University of Wisconsin (M.A., Litt.D.). A veteran traveler in exotic regions, he has written many books on Mexico, the South Seas, etc. His eighth volume of poetry, *Tropic Earth*, appeared in 1944. He is a native of Milton Junction, Wis.

GIBRAN, KAHLIL (1883-1931), Syrian-American mystic, poet and artist, was born in Lebanon. He first visited the United States at the age of twelve, studied art in Paris, and was well known as a poet and playwright at twenty, when he adopted English as his medium of expression. *The Prophet*, a philosophical prose-poem published in Paris in 1926 and in America in 1930, and repeatedly reprinted, achieved a phenomenal success. His biography, written by Barbara Young, appeared in 1945.

GILLESPIE, YETZA was born in Warrensburg, Mo. She studied in the local high school as well as at the State Teacher's College. Her poems have appeared in more than half a hundred periodicals.

GINSBERG, LOUIS is a resident of Paterson, N. J. where, for the past twenty years, he has taught classes in English at the Central High School. He was born in Newark and received his B.A. and M.A. from Rutgers (1918) and Columbia (1924). He has published two books of poems: *The Attic of the Past* (Small, Maynard 1920) and *The Everlasting Minute* (Liveright 1937). His work appears frequently in American, Canadian and British magazines.

GOODMAN, MAE WINKLER spent her childhood on a Louisiana sugar plantation. Born in New Orleans, she has made her home, since 1923, in Cleveland, O. She is a graduate of Western Reserve University. *Foam Against the Sky*, published in brochure form by the American Weave, was the winner of that magazine's award for 1945.

GRIFFITH, WILLIAM (1876-1936) was president of the PSA from 1929 to 1931. He was born in Memphis, Mo. and did journalistic and editorial work in New York City for many years. He is the author of three volumes of verse, among them the popular *Loves and Losses of Pierrot*. He also edited a number of books and anthologies.

GUINEY, LOUISE IMOGEN (1861-1920), native of Boston, spent the last two decades of her life in England. She was a poet of great spiritual integrity, a dedicated artist, who composed lyrics of the first order. Her *Happy Ending*, the last of her five volumes, was reissued in 1937 by the Houghton Mifflin Company.

GUITERMAN, ARTHUR (1871-1943) came to this country from Vienna at the age of three. A graduate of the College of the City of New York, he was one of the few poets who succeeded in making a "vocation of an avocation". He was a versatile writer, adept in poetic drama, occasional verse and balladry, and a popular lecturer. He served the PSA as president for two terms (1925-1927). *The Laughing Muse,* published by Harper in 1915, was one of his earliest and best known volumes of verse. He was also the author of *The Light Guitar* (Harper 1923), *Death and General Putnam* (1935) and *Gaily the Troubadour* (1936), the two last published by Dutton.

GUSTAFSON, RALPH is a native of Lime Ridge, Quebec, now resident in New York City where he is associated with the British Information Service. He is the author of three volumes of poems (among them *Flight into Darkness,* issued by Pantheon Books in 1944) and has edited three widely-read anthologies of Canadian verse.

HAGEDORN, HERMANN studied at Harvard, Columbia, and the University of Berlin. He composed the Harvard Tercentenary Ode in 1936. He is the author of more than a score of works in poetry, prose and drama. He edited the *Memorial Edition of the Works of Theodore Roosevelt* (1923-1925) and wrote the official biography of Edwin Arlington Robinson, published in 1938. His *High Flight,* a memoir of John Magee, poet airman who met his death in World War II, is one of his recent publications. His latest is *Americans,* a book of essays on the lives of famous contemporaries (John Day Company 1946). For many years he was a leading figure in the life of the MacDowell Colony. He was born in New York City and lives in Santa Barbara, Calif.

HALL, AMANDA BENJAMIN (Mrs. John A. Brownell) is a native and resident of Connecticut. She attended private schools in the United States and abroad, and studied fiction and verse technique at New York University and Columbia. She is a winner of PSA and Poetry (Chicago) annual awards. She has three volumes of fiction and five of poetry to her credit. *Unweave a Rainbow,* a book of verse, appeared in 1942 (Decker).

HALL, HAZEL (1886-1924) was born in St. Paul, Minn. but in early childhood moved to Portland, Ore. She was confined to a wheelchair from the age of twelve until her death. In this "narrow room" her *élan vital* unfaltering, she earned a modest living by her fine needlework and enriched the world with three volumes of lyric poetry. *Curtains* appeared in 1921, *Walkers* in 1923, and *Cry of Time* posthumously in 1928.

HAMILTON, MARION ETHEL of San Diego, Cal. is a native of Ripon, Wis. She is a contributor of verse to the Commonweal, Lyric, Voices, Wings, Poetry Chap-Book and elsewhere. *The Ultimate Lover* was published by Pascal Covici in 1927.

HANES, LEIGH is a native of Virginia and holds LL.B., M.A. and Litt.D. degrees from Washington and Lee University. He has published two books of poetry, lectures extensively, and has served as editor of The Lyric since 1929.

HARDY, ELIZABETH STANTON was born in Cleveland, O. and now resides in Rochester, N. Y. She has taught poetry technique at the University of Rochester and elsewhere. She is the author of *Time in the Turning*, published in 1940.

HARE, AMORY started her literary career in 1920 with *Tossed Coins*, a book of poems published by John Lane. This was followed by four additional collections of verse, two plays and a novel. She has also published short fiction in the Mentor, Nash (England), Harper's Bazaar, etc. In 1924 she won the Browning Medal. She is a native of Philadelphia.

HASTE, GWENDOLEN was born in Streator, Ill., and is a graduate of the University of Chicago. She won the Nation poetry prize in 1922. A collection of her poems, *Young Land*, was published by Coward-McCann in 1930. She contributes to many magazines and is represented in more than twenty anthologies. She was secretary of the PSA in 1928-29 and a member of the executive board from 1929 to 1936.

HASTINGS, FANNY de GROOT is a native of Tarrytown-on-Hudson and a present resident of New Canaan, Ct. Her first book was published in 1912 by the Alice Harriman Company under the title *The Victory of Defeat*. In 1917, 1919 and 1921 William Edwin Rudge brought out her *Ten Minutes, Lesser Stars* and *Through a Glass*. A brochure, *From a Barn Window*, appeared in 1928.

HAY, SARA HENDERSON (Mrs. Raymond Holden) of Weston, Conn. is the author of two volumes of poems, *Field of Honor*, which won the 1933 Kaleidograph award, now in its sixth edition, and *This, My Letter*, published in 1939 (Knopf). Her reviews of poetry and fiction appear regularly in the Saturday Review of Literature. She has given many programs of her own work on the lecture platform and over the radio. She is a vice-president of the PSA.

HENDERSON, DANIEL (MAC INTYRE) was born in Baltimore, lives in New York City and has a farm retreat in New Jersey. He is the author of, among other works, *Life's Minstrel* (Dutton 1920), *A Harp in the Winds* (Appleton 1924) and *Frontiers* (Bruce Humphries 1934) and has a new book in preparation. He served several terms as a vice-president of the PSA.

HEYWARD, DUBOSE (1885-1940) was a native of Charleston, S. C. and did most of his work in and about the South. Though he began his career as a poet with the publication of *Carolina Chansons* (with Hervey Allen), his fame rests largely on his novelized portrayals of Negro life, as in *Porgy* and *Mamba's Daughters*. On the dramatization of these works, which were eminently successful in both forms, his wife, Dorothy Heyward, collaborated with him.

HIMMELL, SOPHIE is a Russian now resident in New York City. She is the winner of several PSA monthly awards. A collection of her verse, *Within the Crucible*, was published by the Wings Press in 1938.

HOBSON, DOROTHY was born in Maryland, the daughter of a Baptist minister. In 1934 she received her A.B. with honors from Hunter. She is the founder (1936) and director of The League To Support Poetry. Two volumes of her poems, *Celestial Interim* (1933) and *Let There Be Light* (1943) have been published. She served two terms on the executive board of the PSA.

HOLDEN, MARCIA NICHOLS is a New Yorker by birth and residence. She is a contributor of verse to current magazines and is associated with The League To Support Poetry.

HOLDEN, RAYMOND was born in New York City, studied at Princeton, and makes his home in Weston, Conn. His third volume of poems, *The Arrow at the Heel*, was brought out by Holt in 1940. He is the author of several novels and a biography of Abraham Lincoln, and is on the staff of the Book-of-the-Month Club.

HOWARD, FRANCES MINTURN makes her home in New York City, hailing originally from Boston. She was educated in private schools here and abroad. At the English Academy in Rome she studied sculpture. Her poems have appeared in the Saturday Review of Literature, Contemporary Poetry, Voices and other periodicals.

HUGHES, DOROTHY BERRY is a graduate of Barnard and the Columbia School of Library Service. She is now a librarian at the New York Public Library. She is a native of St. Louis, Mo. Her work appears in many of the country's leading journals of verse.

JACOBSEN, JOSEPHINE is a Baltimorean in the Winter and a resident of New Hampshire in the Summer. She is the author of *Let Each Man Remember* (1940) and *For the Unlost,* fourth of the Contemporary Poetry Distinguished Poets Series (1946).

JENNINGS, LESLIE NELSON was born in Ware, Mass. His early years were spent in California where he was a protege of George Sterling. He returned to the East some time later and became associate editor of Current Opinion. His verse has appeared in The New Yorker, Saturday Review of Literature, Poetry, The Nation, The New Republic, etc. He is the author of *Mill Talk & Other Poems* published by The Fine Editions Press in 1942.

JOHNS, ORRICK, one of the pioneers of the "new poetry" in America, hails from St. Louis, Mo. He studied at the University of Missouri and at Washington University, and served as dramatic critic and book reviewer for Reedy's St. Louis Mirror. In 1912 his poem "Second Avenue" won the Lyric Year first prize of $500. His published work includes *Asphalt & Other Poems* (Knopf 1917), *Black Branches* (Pagan Publishing Co. 1920), *Blindfold,* fiction, (Lieber & Lewis 1923), and *Time of Our Lives,* the story of his father's and his own life (Stackpole Sons 1937). In 1936 he was director of the Federal Writers' Projects in New York City.

JOHNSON, JOSEPHINE of Norfolk, Va. is an honorary Phi Beta Kappa member of the College of William and Mary. The Kaleidograph

Press brought out *The Unwilling Gypsy*, a collection of her verse, in 1936. She shares with Mary Sinton Leitch the presidency of the Poetry Society of Virginia.

JOHNSON, VICTORIA SAFFELLE is a graduate (1945) of the University of California. She lives in Berkeley and was born in Santa Rosa. Her chief interests are modern languages, ornithology, and poetry.

JONES, LEILA is a resident of Fairfield, Conn. She contributes to leading literary journals and is the author of two volumes of poems, *Assent to Autumn* (1933) and *Winter Is a Shadow* (1939).

JONES, MARY HOXIE, a Pennsylvanian by birth and residence, received her B.A. from Mt. Holyoke College. She has published two volumes of prose and a collection of poems, *Arrows of Desire* (Macmillan 1931).

JONES, RUTH LAMBERT was born in Haverhill, Mass. and is still a resident of that city. She is a graduate of Bradford Academy. Her work in verse and prose has appeared in many periodicals and anthologies.

JONES, THOMAS S., JR. (1882-1932), one of America's most distinguished religious poets, was born in up-state New York and attended Cornell University. He made his home for the most part in New York City where he did editorial work for the New York Times. He published ten volumes of poetry. *The Rose Jar*, one of his best known collections, has gone into many editions.

KAHN, HANNAH is a New Yorker by birth, now residing in Miami, Fla. Her poems have appeared in The Lyric, Florida Magazine of Verse, Voices, and other poetry journals.

KENT, LUCY is a native New Yorker. A section in *New Poets* (Decker 1941) is devoted to her work. She has read over WOR and other radio stations, and has a volume of poems in preparation.

KILMER, ALINE (1888-1941), wife of Joyce Kilmer and mother of Kenton Kilmer, was born in New Jersey. Her first book, *Candles That Burn* (Doubleday & Co.) appeared after the death of her husband. She was the author of three volumes of verse. Her *Selected Poems* appeared in 1929.

KILMER, JOYCE (1886-1918) was born and educated in New Jersey. He taught school for a time and did editorial work on various journals. His poem Trees, which appeared in 1913, brought him national fame. During World War I he was a popular lecturer and "belletristic journalist." In 1917 he enlisted and died in action in France the following year. His collected works were published in two volumes in 1918 under the title *Joyce Kilmer, Edited, with a Memoir, by Robert Cortes Holliday* (Doran).

KINSOLVING, SALLY BRUCE of Richmond, Va. is the founder of the Poetry Society of Maryland and the author of four books of verse, among them *Depths and Shallows* (1921) and *Grey Heather* (1930). In 1941 the Enoch Pratt Library of Baltimore created the Sally Bruce Kinsolving Collection, comprising letters by contemporary American and English poets. She has lectured widely and is a Phi Beta Kappa member.

KONOPAK, FARONA was born in Philadelphia, lived in New Mexico for many years, and now resides in Toledo, O. She has contributed to various publications, and is the author of one book of poems, *Adobe in Sunlight* (Galleon Press 1935).

KREYMBORG, ALFRED, past president of the PSA (1943-1944), was born in New York City. He has published more than forty volumes in poetry and prose and has contributed to leading experimental magazines, several of which he founded or edited: Musical Advance, The Glebe, Others, Broom, The American Caravan (the last with Lewis Mumford and Paul Rosenfeld). He has given courses in poetry at the New School, Briarcliff Junior College, Olivet College, Bread Loaf School of English, etc., and has lectured at Oxford. His most recent publication is his *Selected Poems 1912-1944* issued by Dutton. The same firm is scheduling for early publication his *Man and Shadow*, a symphonic poem.

KRUGER, FANIA of Wichita Falls, Tex. is a native of Sevastopol, Russia. She attended Russian gymnasia and has taken courses at Harvard and Columbia. She is the author of *Cossack Laughter* (Kaleidograph Press 1937).

LAING, ALEXANDER was born on Long Island and resides in Norwich, Vt. with his poet wife, Dilys Bennett Laing, and their young son. He studied at Dartmouth (B.A.), was a Guggenheim Fellow in 1934-1935, and since 1937 has held the post of assistant librarian of Dartmouth. Author of a dozen and more books in prose and poetry, he is an authority on clipper ships. A new edition of his epic of the clipper era, *The Sea Witch*, appeared in 1944. His most recent work in the field is *Clipper Ship Men*, published by Duell, Sloan & Pearce in 1945.

LAWRENCE, GORDON teaches biology at Walton High School in New York City. He is editor of *The Teaching Scientist* and the author of *My Horses are Grasshoppers*, the latter a volume of poetry, published by the Chisholm Press in 1929. He hails from New Orleans.

LECHLITNER, RUTH (Mrs. Paul Corey) was born in Wakarusa, Ind. and received B.A. and M.A. degrees from the universities of Michigan and Iowa. Her first book of poems, *Tomorrow's Phoenix*, appeared in 1937; her second, *Only the Years,* in 1945. Her reviews of contemporary poetry appear regularly in the New York Herald Tribune Sunday book section. She makes her home in Cold Springs-on-Hudson, N. Y.

LEGALLIENNE, RICHARD, charter member of the PSA, was born in England and educated principally at Liverpool College. Early in life he abandoned a business career for literature and for some years lived and wrote in the United States. He now resides in Mentone, France. He is the author of more than two score works in poetry, drama and belles lettres. *Pieces of Eight* (1940) is his most recent book. Among the titles he has edited are Izaak Walton's *The Compleat Angler,* Hazlitt's *Liber Amoris,* and Hallam's *Remains.* His daughter, Eva, is the noted actress.

LEGEAR, LAURA LOURENE hails from Waco, Tex. and resides in Flushing, N. Y. She is the winner of many poetry awards. Her poems have appeared in the Saturday Review of Literature, Poet Lore, New York Times, etc.

LEITCH, MARY SINTON of Lynnhaven, Va. was born in New York City. She received her education at Smith College, Columbia University, and in schools abroad. She is co-president of the Poetry Society of Virginia and an honorary member of Phi Beta Kappa. Her published works include four volumes of poetry, a translation of the *Love Letters of Bismarck,* and an anthology, *Lyric Virginia Today.* She was awarded the PSA second prize for 1945.

LEMONT, JESSIE (Mrs. Lemont Trausil) is a native of Louisville, Ky. but has resided in New York City for the greater part of her life. Widely known for her translations of Rainer Maria Rilke, whose work she was the first to introduce to the English-speaking public, she is the author of two volumes of her own poems, *White Nights* (Mosher 1930) and *Where Stillness Lies the Deepest* (The Fine Editions Press 1944).

LEONARD, WILLIAM ELLERY (1876-1944) studied at Harvard and in European institutions of learning. In 1906, on his return to the United States, he joined the faculty of Wisconsin University. He published more than a dozen books of poetry and translations, including a free verse rendering of the Babylonian epic *Gilgamesh.* His outstanding achievement was the intense and moving novel in sonnet form, *Two Lives* (1925). A self-analytical prose work, *The Locomotive God,* appeared in 1927, and a posthumous volume, *A Man Against Time,* a love story in sonnet sequence, was published by Appleton-Century late in 1945. He was born in Plainfield, N. J. and died in Madison, Wis.

LEWIS, MAY (Mrs. Lafayette Goldstone) is a native New Yorker and attended Columbia University. She has lectured widely on modern poetry, has done considerable editorial work for special magazines, and has published one volume of poems, *Red Drumming in the Sun* (Knopf 1931).

LIEBERMAN, ELIAS was born in St. Petersburg, Russia. He received his B.A. cum laude from the College of the City of New York in 1903 and his M.A. in 1906 and Ph.D. in 1911 from New York University.

He is the author of *Paved Streets* (1918), *The Hand-Organ Man* (1930), *Man in the Shadows* (1939), and editor of *Poems for Enjoyment* (1932), an anthology-guide to poetry appreciation. Under his direction *Moments of Enchantment,* a collection of work done by junior high school pupils, was compiled. His "I Am an American" (Everybody's Magazine, July 1916) gave the name and the stimulus to the current "I Am an American" celebrations throughout the country. He is an associate superintendent of schools in New York City. He has served the PSA as a vice-president and member of the executive board.

LINDBERGH, ANNE MORROW is a B.A. and honorary M.A. of Smith College. In 1933 she was the recipient of the United States Flag Association's award for her part in surveying transatlantic air routes. A year later she received the Hubbard gold medal of the National Geographic Society for her work as radio operator and co-pilot with her husband, Charles A. Lindbergh, on their epic-making global flight. She is the author of four volumes of prose, the most recent, *The Steep Ascent,* published by Harcourt, Brace in 1944.

LINDSAY, NICHOLAS VACHEL (1879-1931) was a native of Springfield, Ill. Early in life he studied art in Chicago and New York. During long walking trips, as minstrel and evangel, he chanted and distributed his *Rhymes to Be Traded for Bread.* In 1914, with the rhythmic and stunning *Congo,* a poem of the Negro, he added to the laurels won with his first volume, *General William Booth Enters Heaven.* He continued to travel about the country (no longer on foot!), while his audiences grew in size and enthusiasm, until the breakdown of his health. Always the crusader, his vision was a living culture for all people. His *Collected Poems* appeared in 1923.

LINK, CAROLYN WILSON of Scarsdale, N. Y., a native of Newark, N. J., is a Vassar alumna. She is the author of *Fir Trees and Fireflies* (Putnam 1921) and *There Is Still Time,* the 1945 prize volume of The League to Support Poetry.

LINK, GORDDEN is at present on active duty with the U. S. Army in the China-Burma-India theatre of operations. By profession he is an instructor of English. His poetry and translations have appeared in such magazines as Asia, Golden Book, Poetry, Saturday Review, etc.

LITSEY, SARAH has contributed to Scribner's, Poetry, McCall's, Collier's, etc. She is the author of one book of poems, *For the Lonely* (Favil Press, London) and a novel, *There Was a Lady* (Bobbs-Merrill). She was born in Springfield, Ky.

LLOYD, ANNE (Mrs. T. M. Lloyd) was born in Brooklyn Heights, N. Y. She has published three books of poems, *Antiques and Amber* (Derrydale Press 1928), *Brief Procession* (Putnam 1934) and *Sight and Sound* (The Fine Editions Press 1944).

LOWELL, AMY (1874-1925) was one of a long line of illustrious Lowells. The poet, James Russell Lowell, was a cousin of her grandfather; Abbott Lawrence Lowell, president of Harvard, was her brother. After a period of study and travel, Miss Lowell turned her mind to poetry. She was then twenty eight. Her first book, *A Dome of Many-colored Glass* (1912), was the forerunner of a rapid succession of volumes, each winning wide critical notice. She identified herself with various avant-garde movements in poetry, particularly with the Imagists, whose reputation she catapulted into fame through her dynamic energy and crusading spirit. During her lifetime she exercised an almost autocratic authority in matters literary. Shortly before her death she completed her monumental work on Keats. Her posthumous volume, *What's O'Clock,* was awarded the Pulitzer prize for poetry in 1926.

LUNDBERGH, HOLGER was born and educated in Stockholm, Sweden, and came to the United States in 1919, settling in New York City. He wrote his first poem in English six years later. More than one hundred seventy five of his poems have since appeared in American periodicals. He is associate director of the American-Swedish News Exchange.

LUTZ, GERTRUDE MAY of Berkeley, Cal. began the serious study of poetry in 1942. She has since contributed to many national magazines, including Accent, American Mercury, Voices, Contemporary Poetry, etc.

MABBOTT, MAUREEN COBB (Mrs. Thomas Ollive Mabbott) hails from Bogard, Mo. She received her Ph.B. and M.A. degrees from the University of Chicago. The Antioch Press published *Crooked Rows,* a volume of her poems, in 1934. She is also the author of two works in bibliography.

MACKAYE, CHRISTY is the daughter of Percy MacKaye and the wife of Henry Barnes. She studied at various private schools in the United States and abroad. *Out of Chrysalis* (Angel Alley Press) and *Wind in the Grass* (Harper) are two of her published works. The latter has an introduction by Edwin Arlington Robinson. She recently returned to New York after an extended stay in Porto Rico.

MACKAYE, PERCY, son of Steele MacKaye, is a resident New Englander, born in New York City. He was educated at Harvard and Leipsig universities, holds several honorary degrees, is a member of the Harvard Phi Beta Kappa, National Institute of Arts and Letters, P.E.N., and other literary organizations. He received the Shelley Memorial award in 1942. He is the author of more than seventy published volumes, including plays in verse, masques and poetic drama. His most recent collection of poems, *My Lady Dear, Arise!,* dedicated to his wife and fellow poet, was issued by Macmillan. He is a charter member of the PSA.

MADELEVA, SISTER MARY (Mary Evaline Wolff) was born in Cumberland, Wis. She is a teacher, lecturer, college president, and the author of eleven books. She holds degrees from five educational institutions. Macmillan brought out her *Selected Poems* in 1942.

MARKHAM, EDWIN (1852-1940), who gained national fame with his epochal poem, The Man With the Hoe, published originally in a San Francisco newspaper at the turn of the century, was born in Oregon, educated in California, and came East in his late forties to settle in New York. His home on Staten Island became a shrine, even during his lifetime, for poets, writers, and champions of social justice. While he wrote innumerable poems, he never equalled the striking power of his first, except perhaps in his *Lincoln, The Man of the People*, one of the noblest tributes in verse to the Great Commoner. In his seventy-fifth year he completed the compilation of a 3,000 page anthology, *The Book of Poetry*. At the time of his death he was Honorary President of the PSA.

MARSHALL, LENORE G. is a native New Yorker and a graduate of Barnard College. *No Boundary*, a collection of her poems, was published by Holt in 1943. She is also the author of two novels, both published by Macmillan. Recent work of hers has appeared in Poetry, Partisan Review, Saturday Review of Literature, and in Cross Section, an anthology of new writing.

MAXWELL, GILBERT was born in Washington, Ga. He was a special scholarship student in creative writing and dramatics at Rollins College. In a varied career he has been, successively, actor, manuscript reader, publicity director, and editor. He is now with the National Broadcasting Company and lives in New York City. *Look to the Lightning* (1933) and *Stranger's Garment* (1936) were both published by Dodd, Mead. His third volume of verse, *The Dark Rain Falling*, appeared in 1942 under the Decker imprint.

McCORD, DAVID of Cambridge, Mass. was graduated from Harvard in 1922 with an M.A. in literature. He began his career as a writer with critical reviews in the Boston Transcript. His first published volume revealed him as a penetrating essayist, his second as a serious poet, his third as an able versifier in light vein. *And What's More*, published in 1941, is a collection in the last-named medium. A popular anthology of American and British humorous verse, *What Cheer*, was brought out by Coward-McCann in 1945.

McCORMICK, VIRGINIA TAYLOR, president and one of the founders of the Poetry Society of Virginia, was born in Berryville, Va. She is the author of several books of verse, including *Winter Apples*, published by Putnam in 1942.

MEARS, ALICE MONKS is a graduate of Oberlin College, is married and the mother of two children. A first book of poems, *Brief Enterprise*, which won the 1945 award of The League to Support Poetry, was published the same year by Dutton. She is also the winner of the Lola Ridge Memorial prize for 1944. She was born in West Chester, Pa. and lives in Narberth, Pa.

MEEKER, MARJORIE of St. Augustine, Fla., the wife of General Vivian Collins, Adjutant General of Florida, was born in England while her father was serving there as American Consul General. In the early 20s, Harriet Monroe awarded her the Young Poet's prize for her *Memorial Sonnets for Cam.* She is the author of *Color of Water,* published by Brentano.

MEYER, GERARD PREVIN was born in New York City. He holds B.A. cum honoribus and M.A. degrees from Columbia. His second collection of poems, *Louder Than the Drum,* was the 1943 prize volume of The League to Support Poetry. He lives in Jackson Heights, N. Y.

MILLAY, EDNA ST. VINCENT achieved fame at nineteen with her long poem "Renascence" which Mitchell Kennerley published first in the Lyric Year and later in her initial volume *Renascence & Other Poems.* After graduating from Vassar she came to New York, joined the Provincetown Players, and became identified with the creative life of Greenwich Village, then at high tide. In 1923 she won the Pulitzer prize with her *The Ballad of the Harp-Weaver.* Her most recent collection of poetry is *Make Bright the Arrows* (Harper 1940). She received the PSA medal in 1943. In private life she is the wife of Eugen Jan Boissevain. She was born in Rockland, Me. and makes her home in Austerlitz, N. Y.

MILLER, JOAQUIN (1841-1913) was born in a covered wagon going West, and remained a picturesque character all his life. In his youth he lived with the Indians, went to a mission school, and prospected for gold. His first published works meeting with little favor, he went to London, launched his poems at his own expense and became a literary lion overnight. After years of travel and three ventures in matrimony, he returned to the United States and founded, in California, a Greek academy for writers. His *Complete Poetical Works* was published by Harr Wagner Publishing Company. He was a charter member of the PSA.

MILLER, MARY OWINGS holds degrees from Winthrop College and the University of South Carolina. She lives in Baltimore, where she edits Contemporary Poetry, a quarterly magazine of verse. She is the author of two books of her own poetry: *Sand Dunes & Other Poems* (1935) and *Only Brown Stubble* (1937) and publishes the work of other poets under the Library Series and Distinguished Poets Series imprints. She is a native of Columbia, S. C.

MINER, VIRGINIA SCOTT of Kansas City, Mo. was born in Lebanon, Ind. and graduated from Northwestern University. She is a teacher and a teacher's wife. The Lantern published her prize book of verse, *Many-Angel River,* in 1938.

MIRICK, EDITH is a native of Washington, D. C. She studied literary technique at George Washington University and playwriting at Catholic University. Her second book of poems, *These Twinkling Acres,* a collection of sonnets, was published in 1935 by the Kaleidograph Press.

MONROE, HARRIET (1860-1936), who made her native city (Chicago) as famous for poetry as it is for stockyards, made her literary debut with *The Columbian Ode,* which was read and sung at Chicago's

Columbian Exposition in 1893. In 1911 she founded and assumed the editorship of Poetry: A Magazine of Verse, the pioneer poetry magazine of America. Always an active and progressive editor, she found time to write a number of volumes of poetry and critical prose, and an autobiography, *A Poet's Life,* which Macmillan published in 1938. She died while visiting South America in the interest of the art to which she had devoted her life.

MONTGOMERY, VAIDA STEWART (Mrs. Whitney Montgomery) was born in Childress, Tex. Her published works include *Locoed & Other Poems* (1930) and *A Century with Texas Poets and Poetry* (1934), both issued under the Kaleidograph Press imprint.

MORGAN, EDWIN is a graduate of New York University and attended the Columbia Graduate School and the Sorbonne in Paris. He edited Daudet's *Lettres de mon Moulin* (Doubleday & Co. 1932) and is the author of *Flower of Evil, A Life of Charles Baudelaire* (Sheed & Ward 1943). He lives in Rockville Centre, L. I.

MORROW, HELEN (Mrs. George Pinkley) was born in Illinois and resides in New York City. She has studied and traveled extensively abroad. Twice a winner of the PSA annual first prize, she is represented in several anthologies.

MORTON, DAVID was professor of English at Amherst for a score of years until he retired in 1945 to devote himself entirely to writing and lecturing. He is the author of an impressive number of books in poetry and criticism and has edited many verse anthologies. He gained fame early in life as a sonneteer. He was born in Elkton, Ky., lives in Amherst, Mass. and recently married. The latest collection of his work, *Poems: 1920-1945,* was published by Knopf.

MURTON, JESSIE WILMORE (Mrs. John Archibald) was educated in Kentucky and Tennessee schools. She has contributed verse to more than two hundred periodicals and is the author of one book of poems, *Frankincense and Myrrh* (1939). She is a native of Kirksville, Ky.

NELSON, STARR was born on Long Island and studied violin at the Ithaca Conservatory of Music. She lives in New York City and is the wife of an artist. Her first book of poems, *Heavenly Body,* was a prize volume of the League To Support Poetry (1942). A new collection, *The Man on the Earth,* is in preparation.

NICHOLL, LOUISE TOWNSEND is of an old New York family. A Smith College graduate, she has published two volumes of poems, *Water and Light* (1939) and *Dawn in Snow* (1941), and a work in prose, *The Blossom Print* (1938). Her work as associate editor of E. P. Dutton & Company now includes direction of all poetry publications issued by that firm. She is a member of the executive board of the PSA.

NORTON, GRACE FALLOW of Sloatsburg, N. Y. is the author of five volumes of poetry (all published by Houghton, Mifflin Co.) and the translator of two prose works. *Little Gray Songs from St. Joseph's* was her first offering and appeared in 1912. It was followed by *The Sister of the Wind* (1914), *Roads* and *What Is Your Legion?* (both in 1916) and the *Miller's Youngest Daughter* (1924).

O'HARA, JOHN MYERS (1874-1944) revealed the influence of Greek literature in all his work. His first book of poems, *At Erato's Fane,* appeared in 1908. *His Pagan Sonnets,* published by Smith & Sale in 1910, was reissued in 1923 and again in 1930. He was the first to translate into English the sonnets of José de Hérèdia. Other translations of his include an "interpretative" edition of Sappho.

OPPENHEIM, JAMES (1882-1932) lived most of his life in New York City where he was a settlement worker, superintendent of a technical school for girls, professional psychoanalyst, short story writer, poet, novelist, and editor of The Seven Arts, one of the pioneering journals in "art for art's sake." Louis Untermeyer points out that all of Oppenheim's poetry was a diagnosis of "the tortured soul of man." He was the author of a score of books in verse and prose, among them *Songs for the New Age* and *War and Laughter,* both published by the Century Company.

O'SHEEL, SHAEMAS was born James Shields, in Greenwich Village, New York City, where he still resides. His interest in Irish literature, the Gaelic Revival and Irish independence caused him to revive the family name of O'Sheel and to transliterate James into its Irish original. Poems from two early collections of his verse, *The Blossomy Bough* (1911) and *The Light Feet of Goats* (1915) were later included in *Jealous of Dead Leaves* (Boni & Liveright, 1928). In 1932 his redaction of the *Antigone* of Sophocles was produced by the New York School of the Theatre and subsequently put on the air by the Radio Guild of NBC. It was the first Greek drama to receive radio presentation.

PALMER, WINTHROP is the author of books in dance criticism, poetry, ballet and fiction. In 1945 two books of hers appeared simultaneously: *Theatrical Dancing in America After 1900* (Bernard Ackerman) and *The Invisible Wife & Other Poems* (The Fine Editions Press). She has two novels scheduled for publication in 1946. An indefatigable writer, mother of three children, associate editor of Voices, she still finds time to seek out and encourage talent in others. She is a resident of New York City.

PEABODY, JOSEPHINE PRESTON (1874-1922) wrote and published verse in early girlhood. She was born in Brooklyn, N. Y. but after 1900 made her home in Cambridge, Mass. where her husband was a professor at Harvard. Although invalided during the last years of her life, she continued to write, chiefly poetic dramas. She was the author of fourteen volumes of poems and plays. Her diary, which she kept from the age of sixteen until her death, was published in 1925. She was a charter member of the PSA.

PERCY, WILLIAM ALEXANDER (1885-1942) owned a plantation estate on the Mississippi delta. He taught, briefly, at Sewanee and, from 1911 on, devoted himself chiefly to the writing of poetry. During

World War I he served at the front as a captain of infantry, winning the Croix de Guerre and other citations. After much travel abroad, particularly in Greece, he returned to Greenville, his native town, to work in the interest of the "poor whites" and negroes of the delta. His autobiography, *Lanterns on the Levee,* appeared in 1941 and his *Collected Poems* posthumously in 1943.

PULSIFER, HAROLD TROWBRIDGE is a past president of the PSA (1931-1932). He was born in Manchester, Conn. and resides in East Harpswell, Me. He holds A.B. and Litt.D. degrees from Bates College and Harvard. His sixth volume of poems, *Rowen,* was published by Houghton Mifflin in 1937. His poetry has been recorded in the Harvard Vocarium Series.

QUARLES, EDWIN (1880-1932) was, during his lifetime, overshadowed as a poet by his *alter ego,* Edwin Latham Quarles, prominent executive member of many civic organizations in various cities of his native state, Virginia. He served as Secretary of the Petersburg, Va. Chamber of Commerce, Director of the Baltimore Commission, Secretary of the Southern Commercial Congress, etc. His lone volume *Poems by Edwin Quarles* was published posthumously and reveals true lyric wit and sensibility. This was a poet who, to quote from one of his own poems, "knew the twice of all he put to speech."

RANDALL-MILLS, ELIZABETH hails from St. Louis, Mo. She was graduated from Vassar (1928) where she edited the Vassar Review. Her poems have appeared in the Virginia Quarterly Review, American Mercury, Poetry, and other magazines.

REECE, BYRON HERBERT came to wide critical notice recently with the publication of his *Ballad of the Bones & Other Poems* (Dutton 1945). He is also the author of *Not the Full Harvest* (Wagon & Star 1944) and is represented with a selection of his work in *Three Lyric Poets,* published by the Press of James A. Decker. He is a native of Choestoe, Ga., and resides in Blairsville in the same state.

REESE, LIZETTE WOODWORTH (1856-1935) was a teacher in the public schools of Baltimore for forty-five years. On her retirement in 1923 from the city's Western High School, the student body, faculty members and alumni presented to the school a bronze tablet inscribed with her famous sonnet, "Tears." She wrote many volumes of poems, all "in praise of common things," in a crisp, lyric vein uniquely her own. Mosher published her *A Wayside Lute* in 1909. Her reminiscenses, *A VictorianVillage,* appeared in 1929. She was a charter member of the PSA.

RICE, CALE YOUNG (1872-1943) was Kentucky born and educated at Cumberland and Harvard. In 1902 he married Alice Hegan, author of the famous *Mrs. Wiggs of the Cabbage Patch.* His work, predominantly philosophical, is contained in more than thirty volumes of poetry, drama and prose. His autobiography, *Bridging the Years,* appeared in 1939. *The Best Poetic Work of Cale Young Rice,* a posthumous collection, was published in 1943 by the Cumberland University Press. He was a charter member of the PSA.

RICHARDS, ROSA COATES is a native of New Orleans, resident in New York City. After an early career as a professional dancer she turned to writing. She is the author of two volumes of verse, *Roadways* and *Skyways*.

RICHTER, MARGARET R. of Los Angeles, Cal. was born in Ohio. She received B.A., M.A. and Ph.D. degrees from Stanford University. Her *Elegy for a Lost Continent*, which appears in this anthology, won second prize in the Lola Ridge Memorial award in 1943. She is an English instructor by profession, and conducts a column in The Matrix, a magazine for women journalists.

RITTENHOUSE, JESSIE B. (Mrs. Clinton Scollard) was one of the moving spirits in the founding of the PSA and the Pulitzer prize for poetry. She is noted for her many anthologies of verse, particularly her *Little Book of Modern Verse* series. She is the author of four volumes of her own poetry, and an autobiography, *My House of Life* (Houghton, Mifflin 1934). Rollins College conferred on her the Litt.D. degree. A native of Mt. Morris, N. Y., she resides in Winter Park, Fla.

ROBERTSON, CLYDE of Denver, Colo., was born in Franklin, Ind., and was educated at Lyons, Kansas High School. After a career in light opera, she took up writing, and is the author of four books of poetry. The latest, *The Yellow Witch*, was published by Loker Raley in 1940. She is a charter member of the Poetry Society of Colorado.

ROBINSON, EDWIN ARLINGTON (1869-1936) is known as one of our great triumverate of New England poets. He spent his boyhood in Gardiner, Me., the "Tilbury Town" of his poems. His first collection, *The Torrent and the Night Before*, was printed at his own expense and appeared in 1896. His subsequent vicissitudes in New York came temporarily to an end when, in 1904, through the efforts of President Theodore Roosevelt, who championed his work, he was given a post at the Customs House. From 1911 until his death he was able, financially, to devote his entire time to poetry, working summers under ideal conditions at the MacDowell Colony in Peterborough, N. H. Volume after volume came steadily from his pen. In 1922, 1925 and again in 1928 he was awarded the Pulitzer prize for his *Collected Poems, The Man Who Died Twice,* and *Tristram.* The latter became an outstanding success. His later, more somber yet richly involved psychological portraitures were more characteristic of his general work. He is, as Ben Ray Redman has said, "a biographer of souls." His last book, *King Jasper,* was completed shortly before his death. In 1942 Macmillan brought out a one-volume edition of his collected work.

ROBINSON, HENRY MORTON, a native of Brooklyn, was educated at Columbia University (B.A., M.A.), where he later became instructor in English literature. In 1925-27 he edited Contemporary Verse. Since 1935 he has been an editor of Reader's Digest. He is the author of ten books, among them *Stout Cortez, Buck Fever* and *Second Wisdom.* His most recent work is a novel, *The Perfect Round* (Harcourt, Brace

1945). He saw active service as gunner's mate in the U. S. Navy in World War I. He makes his home in Woodstock, N. Y.

RORTY, JAMES was born in Middletown, N. Y. and educated at Tufts College. He worked as an advertising writer in California and New York (with excursions into radical journalism) until 1931, when he retired to a farm near Westport, Conn. His only volume is *Children of the Sun,* published in 1926.

ROSENBERGER, COLEMAN, of Washington, D. C., is a member of the Virginia bar. He is the author of *The Virginia Poems,* and has contributed articles, poetry and reviews to The Nation, New Republic, Poetry, Voices, Yale Poetry Review, and other publications.

ROSS, DAVID is a native New Yorker and a pioneer in poetry readings on the radio. His *Poet's Gold* anthology, first published in 1933, was reissued in 1945 in a new and enlarged edition (Dial Press).

RUSSELL, SYDNEY KING is the author of seven published books of verse, among them *Lost Warrior* (Mosher 1931), *Proud Universe* (Putnam 1940) and *Songs for America* (The Fine Editions Press 1943). He is the composer of many concert songs, one of which, Harbor Night, won the Kimball award in 1945. He is an editor of the Poetry Chap-Book and a member of the executive board of the PSA.

SALOMON, I. L. was born in Hartford, Conn., resides in New York, and claims Vermont as his second home. Much of his poetry deals with the way of life in the Green Mountain State. His work appears in Contemporary Poetry, Encore, Poetry Chap-Book, etc. He holds B.A. and M.S. degrees from the College of the City of New York.

SAMPSON, HARRIET was born in Woodstock, Conn. She received her education at Wellesley (B.A.), and has done graduate work in 15th century literature at Columbia. She is co-author of *A Girl of the Eighties* (Houghton, Mifflin 1931) and edited John Evelyn's *The Life of Mrs. Godolphin* (Oxford University Press, London, 1937).

SANTAYANA, GEORGE was born in Madrid, Spain of Spanish parents, and has lived in Europe since 1914. Brought to Boston as a child, he was educated at Harvard, where he taught philosophy until 1912. It was there that he began his long and celebrated series of philosophical works. His *Sonnets and Poems* appeared in 1894. His own selection from his *Poems* was issued in 1923. His *The Last Puritan,* described by himself as "a memoir in the form of a novel," was published in his seventy-second year and received wide acclaim. *The Middle Span,* the second volume of his autobiography, was one of the literary events of 1945. In the early Spring of 1946 Scribner's published his essay in Christology, *The Idea of Christ in the Gospels.* He is a charter member of the PSA.

SARETT, LEW was born in Chicago and educated at Beloit College (A.B.), the University of Illinois (LL.B.) and Baylor University (Litt.D.). He is the author of five books of poetry, all published by Holt. *The Collected Poems of Lew Sarett* appeared in 1941.

SCHAFFNER, JOHN was born in Wellesley, Mass. and lives in Springfield, O. He was graduated from Bowdoin College in 1935 and has taught in Maine, Virginia and New York City. He was on active duty as ensign in the U. S. Naval Reserve (1942-43), and is at present on the editorial staff of Collier's. He is the author of one collection of poems, *Island Boy* (Bradford Press 1937).

SCOLLARD, CLINTON (1860-1932) was born in Clinton, N. Y. He began his literary career at the age of fourteen when his father gave him a printing press. After graduating from Hamilton College he went to Harvard where he became active as a poet. His travels abroad, particularly in Egypt and Palestine, inspired some of his best work. He has to his credit more than forty books in prose and verse. His selected poems were issued posthumously in 1934 under the title *The Singing Heart,* to which his wife, Jessie B. Rittenhouse, contributed a Memoir. He was a charter member of the PSA.

SCRUGGS, ANDERSON M. was born in West Point, Ga. and resides in Atlanta, where he is Professor at the Dental School of Emory University. He contributes to numerous publications and is the author of two volumes of poems, *Glory of Earth* (Oglethorpe University Press 1937) and *Ritual for Myself* (Macmillan 1941).

SHERMAN, FRANK DEMPSTER (1860-1916) was Professor of Graphics at Columbia University, a genealogist of note, a designer of book-plates, and a poet who specialized in *vers de société* and the brief, graceful lyric. His *Collected Poems* appeared, with an Introduction by his friend, Clinton Scollard, in 1917. He was a charter member of the PSA.

SHERRY, RUTH FORBES, a native of Chicago, now resides in Long Beach, Cal. She was educated at Vassar, Stanford, and the Sorbonne. She has published two volumes of poetry and a brochure, *Lament and Prophecy* (1944). Her work has appeared in more than two hundred periodicals.

SKINNER, CONSTANCE LINDSAY (1882-1939) was born at a Hudson's Bay trading post and spent her childhood among Indians, "mounties" and fur traders. She achieved success not only as a poet but as a widely-known newspaper writer and author of books for children. At the time of her death in New York City she was editor of the *Rivers of America* series.

SMITH, ELEANOR SANDS (Mrs. Ranald Leary Smith) is a native and resident of Benton, Pa. She studied at state teachers colleges in Bloomburg, Pa. and Montclair, N. J., and at Pennsylvania State College. She served as editor of the poetry quarterly, Unicorn (1939-1943).

SPEYER, LEONORA (Mrs. Edgar Speyer) was born in Washington, D. C. After a successful career as concert violinist, she turned to poetry. With her second book, *Fiddler's Farewell* (1926), she won the Pulitzer award. *Naked Heel* followed in 1931 and *Slow Wall* in 1939. The latter work, expanded to include a section of new poems, is on the Spring

1946 list of Knopf, who published her three previous books. Mrs. Speyer is a member of Phi Beta Kappa (honorary) of William and Mary College and is honorary vice-president of the PSA, which she served as president from 1932 to 1934. Since 1938 she has conducted classes in verse-writing and literary criticism at Columbia University.

SPINGARN, LAWRENCE P. is a native of Jersey City, N. J. He studied at Bowdoin College, University of Michigan, Bread Loaf School of English and the New School for Social Research. His first book of poems, *Rococo Summer and Other Poems,* is on the 1947 list of Dutton.

STEARNS, FLORENCE DICKINSON was born in Atlanta, Ga. Her work as critic and poet has appeared in many periodicals. A collection of her poems, *Strange Dimension,* was published by Putnam in 1938. She is president of the Poetry Society of Virginia.

STERLING, GEORGE (1869-1926) spent most of his years in California where, with Ambrose Bierce and Jack London, he was in the vanguard of the San Francisco literary life of the period. In the words of Idwal Jones, he was San Francisco's last classic bohemian. He took his own life, leaving ten volumes of poetry and a host of legends. He was born at Sag Harbor, L. I., and was a charter member of the PSA.

STICKNEY, HELEN FRITH is a native New Yorker. Her first book, *Prelude to Winter,* a prize-winning volume, appeared in 1934 (Banner Press). A second collection of her poems, *Abigail's Sampler,* was issued by The Fine Editions Press in 1943. She is a member of the executive board of the PSA and served as a vice-president in 1943 and 1944.

SULLIVAN, A. M., president of the PSA from 1939 to 1941, was born in Harrison, N. J., and educated at St. Benedict's Preparatory College, Newark. He conducted the Radio Forum of Poetry over the Mutual network from 1932 to 1940. He is associate editor of Dun's Review. His published work includes *Ballad of a Man Named Smith* (Decker 1940), *A Day in Manhattan* (Dutton 1941), *Ballad of John Castner* (The Fine Editions Press 1943) and *Stars and Atoms Have No Size* (Dutton 1946). He is active in many enterprises, literary and business, as organizer, counselor and lecturer.

TANASSO, ELDA of Harrison, N. Y. received her B.A. from the College of New Rochelle and her M.A. in English from Columbia University where she is a member of the English Graduate Union. She also holds a degree in violin from the Grosskopf Conservatory of Music. She is the author of *The Dark Gaze,* a volume of poetry published by Bruce Humphries in 1944, and of several short stories which appeared in Mademoiselle. She was awarded the PSA 1945 first prize for her poem, The Creators.

TARDY, ANNE SOUTHERNE, a resident of Birmingham, Ala., is one of the founders of the Poetry Society of Alabama and is prominent in club circles throughout the state. She is the author of *Sun Through Window Shutters* (Stephen Daye Press 1935).

TAYLOR, MARY ATWATER (Mrs. Henry Taylor) is a Vassar alumna and, while an undergraduate, edited the Vassar Miscellany. She is the winner of a nation-wide prize contest for the best sonnet on Thomas Jefferson. Her published works include *October Orchard* (Maverick Press) and *Ropes and Threads* (Mosher). She served on the executive board of the PSA for a term of five years. She was born in New Haven, Ct., a daughter of the late Dr. John H. Mason of Boston.

TEASDALE, SARA (1884-1933) was born and educated in St. Louis, Mo. After a period of travel in Europe and the Near East, she settled in New York with her husband, Ernst Filsinger. Her first book, *Sonnets to Duse* (1907), proclaimed the advent of a new poet of the first order. Six additional volumes of verse followed, of which *Flame and Shadow* (1920) contained perhaps her best work. She was awarded the first PSA-Pulitzer award in 1918 for her *Love Songs*. The following year she served as one of the judges of this award. She grew steadily in artistry, despite failing health and loneliness that attended her last days.

THOMAS, ROSEMARY was born in Tacoma, Wash. She was graduated from Smith College in 1923. For the past fourteen years she has taught English at the Spence School in New York City. Her poetry has appeared in various magazines.

THOMPSON, DOROTHY BROWN is a native of Springfield, Ill. and lives in Kansas City, Mo. She received her A.B. degree from the University of Kansas. Her work has appeared in more than one hundred periodicals, eleven textbooks and numerous anthologies. A group of her poems has been transcribed in Braille.

TIETJENS, EUNICE (1884-1944) once declared that she was "born under a wandering star." She was educated in Europe and traveled widely, but at twenty-seven returned to Chicago, city of her birth, and was "re-born". She met Harriet Monroe and began her quarter century of association with the magazine Poetry. In 1920 she married Cloyd Head. She published poems, plays, textbooks, juvenile fiction, and in 1938 her autobiography, *The World at My Shoulder*.

TORRENCE, RIDGELY was born in Zenia, O. and educated at Miami University (Litt.D.) and Princeton. He was librarian at the Astor and the Lenox Libraries in New York (1897-1903), and an editor of The New Republic (1920-1934). He was Resident Professor in Creative Writing at Antioch College in 1939 and at Miami University in 1941. He is the author of three volumes of poetry and three volumes of plays, including a group for a Negro Theater. His most recent volume *Poems* (1941) won the Shelley Memorial award. In 1945 he edited the *Last Poems of Anna Hempstead Branch*. He and Mrs. Torrence (Olivia Howard Dunbar) live in Greenwich Village in New York City. He is a charter member of the PSA.

TOWNE, CHARLES HANSON, noted editor and charter member of the PSA, was born in Louisville, Ky. He is the author of seven volumes of verse. The first, *The Quiet Singer,* appeared in 1912; the seventh, *An April Song,* in 1937. His autobiography, *So Far So Good,* reminiscent of a crowded and eventful life among the literati, was published by Messner in 1945.

TUNSTALL, VIRGINIA LYNE of Norfolk, Va. is the author of *A White Sail* (Vinal 1927). She is an honorary member of Phi Beta Kappa, College of William and Mary. She was born in Henderson, Ky. where she received her early schooling.

UNTERMEYER, JEAN STARR is a native of Zanesville, O. and was educated in schools in Ohio and New York. She is the author of five volumes of poetry, including her collected poems *Love and Need* (Viking 1940). In 1928 Dodd, Mead published her translation of *Schubert the Man* from the German of Oscar Bie. Mrs. Untermeyer's most recent work is a translation of the monumental prose-poem, *The Death of Virgil,* by Hermann Broch (Pantheon Books 1945). In 1940 she was appointed to the Ford Madox Ford Chair of Creative Literature at Olivet College. A vice-president of the PSA in 1945, she has also served many terms on the society's executive board.

VINAL, HAROLD, founder and editor of Voices, divides his time between New York City and Vinalhaven, Me., the island of his birth. He spent his early years in Boston where he studied the piano. His interest in poetry stems from the 1920s when his first book, *White April,* was published (1922) followed by *Voyage* (1923), *Nor Youth Nor Age* (1924), *A Stranger in Heaven* (1927), *Hymn to Chaos* (1931) and *Hurricane* (1936), the latter a blank verse book-length chronicle of the Maine coast. His most recent collection of poems, *The Compass Eye,* appeared in 1944. He has served the PSA as secretary for many years.

WALLIS, ELEANOR GLENN is a native of Baltimore. Her first book, *Child on a Mill-Farm,* appeared in 1937 (Kaleidograph Press). Her most recent volume is *Tidewater Country* (Decker 1944). A fourth book of her poems is scheduled for 1946 by Contemporary Poetry in its Distinguished Poets Series.

WARD, MAY WILLIAMS of Wellington, Kan., was born in Holden, Mo. and received her education at the University of Kansas. She was editor of The Harp from 1926 to 1931. Her *Poems for Choral Speaking* (Harvel & Ward) appeared in 1945.

WARREN, JAMES E. JR., a member of the Army Air Corps since 1942, is a native of Atlanta, Ga. He was educated at Emory University (B.A., M.A.) and taught English in Atlanta High School. A winner of the PSA annual prize in 1937, he has published one volume of poems, *This Side of Babylon* (1938).

WEBB, TESSA SWEAZY of Columbus, O. attended Ohio State University and is Financial Secretary of the Agricultural Extension Service of Ohio. Editor of The Singing Quill, founder of Ohio Poetry Day, and tireless promoter of poetry in her native state, she has published two volumes of her own verse, the most recent, *Window by the Sea,* appearing in 1942.

WELLES, WINIFRED (1893-1939) wrote many of her poems in her ancestral home in Norwich Town, Conn., and many of the town's local characters appear in them. After her marriage she moved to New York City. With her first book, *The Hesitant Heart,* her gifts were apparent. She published three succeeding volumes, and in 1944 *The Shape of Memory* appeared, a posthumous collection prefaced by William Rose Benét and with an Introduction by her friend and fellow-poet, Louise Townsend Nicholl. In 1946 Holt published her one prose work, *The Lost Landscape,* an autobiographical memoir.

WHEELOCK, JOHN HALL was born at Far Rockaway, L. I., is a graduate of Harvard and has done post-graduate work at the universities of Göttingen and Berlin. He lives in New York City. His first book, *Verses by Two Undergraduates* (in collaboration with Van Wyck Brooks), appeared in 1905. He has since published seven volumes of poetry, including *Poems, 1911-1936* (Scribner's), and two prose works. In 1939 he compiled and edited *The Face of a Nation: Poetical Passages from the Writings of Thomas Wolfe* (Scribner's). He served as a vice-president of the PSA in 1945.

WIDDEMER, MARGARET is a native of Philadelphia, long resident in New York City. While still a child she won several first prizes in poetry. In 1919 she shared a PSA-Pulitzer award with Carl Sandburg. She won the Saturday Review of Literature award in 1923 for her "Tree with a Bird in It" as the best poetic satire of that year. She is noted also as a novelist and lecturer. Her eight volumes in poetry include *Factories* (Henry Holt 1917), *Ballads and Lyrics* (Harcourt Brace 1923), *Collected Poems* (Harcourt Brace 1928) and *Hill Garden* (Farrar & Rinehart 1936). She is a past and present vice-president of the PSA.

WILKINSON, MARGUERITE (1883-1928) was born in Halifax, N. S. and came to the United States as a child. She published magazine verse while a student at Northwestern University. She lectured widely, served two years as poetry critic on the New York Times and was a devotee of trout fishing. In 1909 she married. Always a liberal, in later years she developed an interest in the early Christian mystics. She wrote a dozen books in verse and prose, including *New Voices,* an analysis of contemporary poetry and poets. As a poet she was an avowed melodist who practiced her own theory of "singing the lyric into life."

WILLIAMS, B. Y. (Mrs. Karl H. Williams), a resident of Cincinnati, O., was born in Hamersville in the same state. Her fourth volume of poems, *For Each a Star,* appeared in 1942. She is co-editor of the poetry quarterly, Talaria.

WOODBERRY, GEORGE EDWARD (1855-1930) was born in Beverly, Mass. of a seafaring family. He attended Harvard, where his senior essay, judged "too pagan in tone" by the college venerables, was privately printed. First known as a Poe authority (despite his dislike of his subject!) he became famous as "The Old Man"—one of the best-loved and most influential professors of English ever to teach at Columbia University. His ex-students organized The Woodberry Society in 1911. He was first and last a poet, John Erskine reminds us, and it was this that made him a great teacher. Author of eighteen volumes in poetry and prose, his *Selected Poems* were brought out in 1933 by Houghton Mifflin Company. He was a charter member of PSA.

WRIGHT, CATHERINE MORRIS (Mrs. Sydney L. Wright) is an artist by profession and studied at the Philadelphia School of Design for Women. She was born in Philadelphia and lives in Wyncote, Pa. She is the author of one volume of poems, *The Simple Nun* (Dorrance 1929).

WRIGHT, FREDERICK A., a native of New York City, resides in Bronxville, N. Y. He received B.A. and B.D. degrees at Columbia University and General Theological Seminary. A winner of the PSA's first prize in 1941, he has published three volumes of poems and a prose work, *St. Augustine's Theology.*

WRIGHT, HELEN M. was born in Brooklyn and lives in Bronxville, N. Y. She was educated at New York University (B.S.) and Columbia University (M.A.).

WRIGHT, MARGARET FREDERICKA, also of Brooklyn, is the daughter of one poet (Frederick A. Wright) and the sister of another (Helen M.). She has won several PSA awards.

WRINN, MARY J. J., a resident of New York City, received B.S. and M.A. degrees from American universities. She studied also at Cambridge University. She is the author of *Elements of Journalism* (revised edition, 1939), *The Hollow Reed,* on the craft and art of writing poetry (1935), and a volume of poems, *Cock on the Ridge* (1940), all published by Harper.

WYLIE, ELINOR (1885-1928) was the granddaughter of a governor of Pennsylvania. She spent her girlhood in Washington, D. C. and part of her young womanhood in England, where her first collection of poems, *Incidental Numbers,* was privately (and anonymously) printed. Ten years later, in America, she made her literary debut with *Nets to Catch the Wind,* achieving immediate recognition. In 1924 she became the wife of William Rose Benét. In the eight years of her literary activity she produced four novels and four volumes of poetry, working in New York, England and the MacDowell Colony at Peterborough, N. H. *Angels and Earthly Creatures* (1929), written at the sustained transcendent height of her powers, was the poet's valedictory volume. Knopf published her collected works in 1932, and in 1943 her *Last Poems* appeared, assembled from various sources by Mr. Benét.

YAUGER, FAY M. of Wichita Falls, Tex. was born in Idaho, and studied at Lindenwood College, Mo. and Emerson College of Oratory, Boston. Her book of poems, *Planter's Charm,* was the 1935 prize volume of the Kaleidograph Press. The title-poem was a winner of the PSA's first prize in 1933.

YOUNG, MARGUERITE is a native of Indiana, now a resident in New York City. The summer she spent on the banks of the Wabash at New Harmony provided the scene and inspiration of her *Angel in the Forest, A Fairy Tale of Two Utopias* (Reynal & Hitchcock 1945). She is the author of two volumes of poems, *Prismatic Ground* (Macmillan 1937) and *Moderate Fable* (Reynal & Hitchcock 1944). She lectured at the Midwestern Writers' Conference at Northwestern University and has a novel in progress.

INDEX OF POEMS

A Considerable Speck   64
A Memorial for Mr. Jefferson   187
A Star by Day   146
A Vagabond Song   31
Abraham Lincoln Walks at Midnight   126
Address to the Doomed   49
American Names   8
An Island   195
And the Days Were Accomplished   56
Answer from Assisi   7
Apology to My Heirs   127
Apostrophe to a Fighter Plane   147
April's Daughter   216
Arcturus in Autumn   210
"As I Came Down from Lebanon"   196
As Though from Love   143
Askew, We Ask You   28
At the Shore   157
Atropos   165
Awake under Stars   93
Awakening   90

Bacchus   198
Bagpipes   167
Bargain   205
Bather Sleeping   221
Behind Dark Spaces   27
Black Sheep   25
Black Soldier   23
Blue Heron   71
Brief Enterprise   148
Broadcast to the Scholars in the Eyrie   188

Camouflage of the Willow Ptarmigan   154
Carpentry   97
Caterpillar   23
Cathedral   30
Cattle Bells   194
Child on the Beach   87
Children on a Hill   80
Clonmacnoise   103
Columbus   153
Come In   65
Concept   136
Confidants   171
Consider, Lord, our Clerk   88
Convent   91
Coral Lizard   86
Coronal: A Legend of the Annunciation   199
Counsel for Youth   208
Cradle Song   168

Credo   109
Crowning   8

David Today   111
Days at Sea   122
Death of the Grandmother   83
Death Stirs the Arras   201
Defeat   27
Deserted   31
Diana Remembers Actaeon   120
Doors   77
Drought   155
Dust   63

Eight Doves   53
Elegy for a Lost Continent   176
Elegy under the Stars   125
Emily Dickinson   72
Encounter   12
End of Farce   185
Epitaph Written in Snow   161
Evening-Mountains   54

Farmer's Wife   16
Fit Remembrance   189
Flammonde   181
Flesh of the Furies   68
Flight into Darkness   75
For a Dancer   95
Foundation   94
Four Little Foxes   194
Freedom Considered   190
From an Ivory Tower   206

Go Down, Moses   108
Golgotha   136
Grecian Lamp Unearthed Near Sparta   233

Hakluyt and the "English Voyages"   35
Harper's Ferry   16
Harvest   101
Harvest Home   213
He Who Loves the Ocean   119
High House   225
House Long Known   15
Human Throne   110
Hunger   41
Hymn to Earth   234
Hymn to Night   29

I Am Desert-Born   157
I Remember   238
I Shall Be Loved as Quiet Things   5
Imperious Design   137
In Space the One Great Ornament   163
In the Beginning Was the Word   18
In Time of Grief   174
In Time of Snow   211

Indian Spring   200
Indian Wife   34
Instant out of Time   78
Invocation   189
Irish Peasant Song   74
It Was Good for the Hebrew Children   145

John   43

Knowing What Time It Is at Night   163

Largo   108
Le Printemps Empoissonné   26
Letter to the City Clerk   231
Lilacs   131
Lincoln, the Man of the People   141
Locket for the Heart   101
Long and Lovely   58
Lost Child   45
Love   70
Love Beleaguered   32
Low Country   99

Man Is Forever Lonely   197
Martyr   94
Midnight Eden   96
Moon Magic   81
Morning without Malice   208
Mortal Hunger   40
Mouse in a Florist's Window   155
Museum Piece   114
My Little Sister   220
My Love and I   138
My Mirror   106

Never Hurt the Proud   226
New Hampshire   211
New York   167
New Wonder   3
No More Poems   104
Notation from Elba   218
Note to "Fiddler's Farewell"   203
November Afternoons   140

O Nations!   55
O World!   192
Ode to Mediterranean   191
Of Foxes   227
Of Little Faith   171
Of One Self-Slain   215
Of Poems   62
Old Age   175
On Becoming a Book   42
On Hearing a Symphony of Beethoven   151
On the Struma Massacre   75
On the Vanity of Earthly Creatures   74
One Black Crow   17
Only the Years   116

Ophidia   85
Oxen   56

Paris   205
Phoenix   164
Pierrette in Memory   73
Pieties   160
Planter's Charm   236
Portrait of Two Unhappy Young People   2
Prayer in an Arctic Season   1
Prayer of a Soldier in France   107
Prevision   103
Prothalamium   214

Quatrains for a Bank Cashier
                                                           49

Refraction   162
Renewal Time   61
Riddles, One, Two and Three   140
Rococo Summer   204

Screech Owls   80
Second Wisdom   184
Short Story   38
Siesta Hour   69
Signature upon Rock   82
Sitting-Room in a Bowery Hotel   124
Skunk Cabbage Rising in March   130
Sleep   89
Small Apocalypse   39
Snow on Avenue B   232
Song Comes Like a Frustrated Flower   13
Song of Starlings   115
Sonnets from "Two Lives"   121
Speech   137
Stains   67
Storm   222
Strawberry Mark   21
Summer Barely Heard   219
Sun through Window Shutters   209

Tasting the Earth   166
The Aristocrat   81
The Arrow's Death   51
The Beasts   87
The Bell-Ringers   185
The Buck in the Snow   152
The Chronometer   207
The Cocks Have Crowed   57
The Crown   83
The Crowning Gift   38
The Dark Chamber   66
The Deaf   128
The Eagle's Song   4
The Funeral   239
The Golden Leopard   40
The Grass   123
The Great Blue Heron   100

The Great Square 51
The Hand 95
The Hawthorn 178
The Little Progress 210
The Magnolia Tree 149
The Mind Has Studied Flight 92
The Most of It 65
The Most Sacred Mountain 212
The Mountain Woman 88
The One Ambassador 22
The Quick Still Center 173
The Raven 240
The Schoolboy Learns to Fly 77
The Secret Heart 37
The Skeleton on the Shore 161
The Stallion 44
The Swan 220
The Two Selves 6
The Two Twilights 222
The Water Ouzel 156
The Weeper 203
The Woods Shall Not Be Lonely 36
The Yellow Witch of Caribou 179
The Zoo in the City 1
There Is a Street 150
These Poems I Have So Loved 202
Third Avenue 114
This Twentieth Century Mind 143
Three O'Clock 214
Threnody 172
To a Wild Goose over Decoys 193
To Alfred Kreymborg 59
To an Ass 44
To Jesus on His Birthday 151
To My Brothers Everywhere 124
Tracks 14
Translation from a Lost Language 68
Travelers in the Orient 230
Tree Toad 97
Tropical Fish 11
Two Deer in a Glade 158
Two North Shore Poems 10
Two Powers 130
Two Sewing 79

Under Glass 109
Unison 223
Unshared Elegy 216

Voyager Man 239

Wandering Child 111
Water Moccasin 118
We Are Wonderful, We Are Wise 24
Weaver 176
Week-End Love 184
What of the Darkness? 117

What Spirit?   148
When a Gull Falls   135
When Bombs on Barcelona Burst   72
When I Am Dead   6
When I Am Ended   58
Whose Eye Is on the Sparrow   174
Wild Apples   46
Wild Duck Song   33
Wild Eden   228
Wild Plum   98
Willow Tree   105
Winter Overture   232

INDEX OF FIRST LINES

A

A prayer is a measureless thing.   22
A speck that would have been beneath my sight   64
A star that burst one afternoon   146
A tank through which you glide and gleam   11
A tiny bell the tree toad has,   97
A touch of nature warms this earthen lamp: 233
A tree grows up by growing down   59
Above the housetops eight doves fly,   53
Across the silken couch of sand   221
Across the years he could recall   37
After split skies and tardy thunder, rain   204
After the hurricane the rocky chasms churned   161
Against the sky a sea bird's breast of cloud,   92
All day the moments gathered for the moment   78
All night long falling from wing-struck air,   176
Ambiguous omens throng the angry sky,
Among the sullen peaks she stood at bay   88
An ivory tower leans against the wind,   206
And the raven takes but a single wife for life,   240
As I came down from Lebanon   196
As I came to the edge of the woods,   65
As shadows slipping along the wall, women   108
Atropos, dread   165

B

Before that ship, there was no motion,   157
Behind him lay the gray Azores,   153
Behold this Easter guest who goes   155
Beneath the flow of words   94
Beware this man who carries in   94
Blacker than black of the plum-tree bough   17

C

Calamus budded in the bottomland,   46
Can you divide seed,   7
Caught in the growing sweep of that design,   176
Come, let us sell the past and future, giving   90
Consider, Lord, our clerk.   88
Corn does not hurry, and the black grape swells   184
Covert and quill lie thick and white as floes   154
Crown us who make within,   8

D

Dark, thinned, beside the wall of stone,   174
Death hath two hands to slay with: with the one   121
Do fishes gleam with hope or flowers feel   109
During the high noon of time,   68

E

Each of my mothers was beautiful,   68
Eagles, leave your sky   188

Enclose the lacquered, coiling snake   1
Enough that you must turn your days to discs   49
Eve, with her warm lips redder   118
Ever the ocean tides, slipping between the islands,   99

F
Farewell, incomparable element,   234
Far-off he heard upon the truce of night   205
Five elms as solid underneath as over   211
For it was winter now,   38
For this your mother sweated in the cold,   151
France must have dogwood, too,   26
Freedom, considered, seems to be   190
From the taut hills, the austere pine   81
From their folded mates they wander far   25

G
"Gee . . . Haw". . . the furrow's deep,   56
Gentian blue as noon-lit sea   199
Gertrude—there's a good old scout!   28

H
Having known other seasons, other faces,   1
He craves a bird's career—   77
He thought he kept the universe alone;   65
He, voyager man, whom old cosmologies framed   239
He who loves the ocean   119
Here at the edge of foam I watch him stand,   87
Here, here among the reeds he stands,   71
Hour after hour, deliberate stroke on stroke,   97
How clear tonight the far jang-jangling bells   194
How far, how far are you faring, April's daughter?   216
How has the dragon shrunken in this age!   86
How is the grass set free?   123

I
I always wanted to make up poems   104
I have fallen in love with American names,   8
I have had courage to accuse;   38
I have heard the wild geese,   175
I heard a sound of voices from the hill   80
I heard the pipes go by   167
I held a fiddle in my hands again,   203
I here; you there—   125
I know a lady, (you know a lady),
I on the thighs of God, as the leaf on the willow!   200
I said, when the word came, 'She will break   171
I saw a fallen sparrow   174
I saw you rise into the sun, trim-lined,   147
I see how the forgetful earth replies,   50
I shall be loved as quiet things   5
I should not want the quarried slate   189
I try to knead and spin, but my life is low the while.   74
I will cross that bridge   103
If I could catch that moth,   109
In a dark hour, tasting the Earth.   166
In a great elm against the winter sky   115
In rooms too-often let, too-meaningly furnished,   184

In space the one great ornament 163
In terror of its own delight 40
In that strange city 41
In the dark days, the early evenings of December, 185
In the green gardens stretched by the green river 220
In the rags of a wind 12
In this world, O scattered man, 195
It is almost forgotten . . . the stepping down from swinging light 83
It is late, I said: there will be a cold rain 239
It is not that the magnolia tree is not beautiful and strange 149
It is portentous, and a thing of state 126
It isn't only where the tall wood ferns 114
It took me ten days 18

L

Leave the thirsting cattle, 213
Let not the white, hot metal of your desire 208
Lifting dark beside the trail 85
Like a young child who to his mother's door 77
Lilacs, 131
Lingers long as time, 45
Listen to the tawny thief 198
Little brown surf- bather of the mountains! 156
Lo, there were giants in old days 114
Long and lovely, cool and white, 58
Long have I heard the rhythm of the sea 108
Lord Gabriel, wilt thou not rejoice 168

M

Man is forever lonely; there can be 197
Minutes were poplars on the avenue 91
Moon of the lost season, linger near, 189
My father rode a horse 238
My little sister had everything 220
My love and I went wandering 139
My love was freshly come from sea 138
My lover is a fool more wise 140
My mother's father's father from his field 127
My shoulders ache beneath my pack 107

N

Nail moonlight to the bark of cherry; 101
Never hurt the proud 226
No autumn woods have wreathed with deepest red 103
No drawing of the planner's art 30
No matter where I turn my head 110
Now are the crops 101
Now as these slaughtered seven hundreds hear 75
Now in your hour of song 111
Now it grows dark. 29
Now lay the hand along the folds of rest, 95
Now more than ever, more than ever now 40
Now the bitter thorn has not 56
Now the doom on land and sea 214
Now they have come, these afternoons in November, 140

O

O lonely trumpeter, coasting down the sky, 193

O Nations! triumphant and vanquished, engrossed with your losses
  and gain,   55
O pitiful and unprotected mind   93
O world, thou choosest not the better part!   192
Of thee the Northman by his beached galley   191
Oh think—the satin-skinned, the dapple,   87
On a train in Texas German prisoners eat   27
On Sunday when the stern bells called for prayer,   34
On the day of this storm there was no sun,   222
On this September night, alone within   51
On this smooth sheet   161
Once every summer, in an emerald light,   80
Once upon a time—once in Georgia—   33
Others knew the lazily-shepherded summer years,   148
Out of the darkness, out of the years, out of the mind's reluctant
  hoardings,   128
Out of the matrix   143

P

Pain is a rat that gnaws away the heart;   124
Paint bites deep   95
Pale is the east with rising sun,   57
Pierrette has gone, but it was not   73
Plow and pasture lie   219
Push up, push up! Your perilous tip   130

R

Reading them over and over   202
Reason, and then all   164
Rejoice, my heart, that the stars do not comprehend you,   171
Remember us, exiles by dead water,   218

S

Salt of the sea was ever on his lips:—   35
Say it is life that matters. Say the bone   49
Scoop a handful of night,   89
Sea shell and flower corolla and strict blade of a wing,   116
See: in the pallid distances, the star   136
She built a house to lock out hate   225
She spoke the dialect of birds,   72
Since you are gone,   205
Sleek from silk water and angled arm. The sun   10
Slowly Nan the widow goes   236
Something immortal is sequestered here   16
Somewhere, behind dark spaces,   27
Song comes like a frustrated flower,   13
Space, and the twelve clean winds of heaven,   212
Speak gently, Spring, and make no sudden sound;   194
Strange, how the moon will come   81
Sun brightens the mating cardinals,   173
Sure-footed, tireless, born to servitude,   44
Sweet sounds. Oh, beautiful music, do not cease!   151

T

Taking him, I understand   16
Test me not for shibboleth;   124
The branch of plum   137
The cactus has its spike,   157

The crusted Tree of stars soars quite   96
The earth is honored, for she keeps your history—   50
The flickering lights men live by in the dark: 160
The forests that were fired by men, return;   61
The grass has come alive.   23
The gray fox for the mountains—   227
The hawthorn in the Devon lanes   178
The heavy hand of afternoon weighs down   69
The hills are high in Caribou,   179
The Honorable the City Clerk: Dear Sir,   231
The jewel-blue electric flowers   214
The little lamp that lit my room   201
The man Flammonde, from God knows where,   181
The night is soundless but its tide has turned—   163
The old house leans upon a tree   31
The pikes of Pennsylvania run   230
The play ends. Children, go home.   185
The polished and proud-necked one,   44
The shadowy hills   54
The snail's small fog-grey silhouette   210
The snow is falling on Avenue B.   232
The sound heard   39
The spring that welled once from this meadow-hill   155
The star went quiet like a sunken bell.   208
The target smiles because   51
The three ghosts on the lonesome road   67
The tusks that clashed in mighty brawls   74
The white marble stands among the mosquitoes   187
The wind is sewing with needles of rain;   79
The wind storms down the desert with more speed,   137
The woods shall not be lonely   36
There are two potent separate powers   130
There is a garden enclosed   228
There is a mirror in my room   106
There is a secret that the sober mood   223
There is a street in town I know   150
There is no privacy in time of snow.   211
There is something in the autumn that is native to my blood—   31
There will be none to chronicle the event,   216
They are unholy who are born   98
They say the jackal and the mole   70
This casual sunlight breaking through with proud   209
This city, all eyes,   167
This is the last refuge I can give you   32
This level ocean, flat and circular   122
This passionate child, so much in love with folly,   2
This place is familiar—   15
This twentieth century mind   143
This was the cross then, O not this solid weight   136
Thrice have I seemed to view Eternity,   83
Time, I am small and easy to defeat,   42
To me, between the all-absorbing wonders   3
Two azure lines traverse the town.   14
Two deer disturbed, alert to an alien sound,   158
Two selves have I that work not for the weal   6

U

Up from a darkness, darker yet,   23
Upon its shadowy edge   62

W

Was it because it was a long summer, the season lived under the tree   21
We are wonderful, we are wise   24
We have fulfilled our apprehension, hope,   75
We walk into the wide embrace   105
W'en de Lawd chose his 'ciples, Peter wuz de fuz',   43
Were I to sleep long sleep, and, pensive, waking,   222
What is the green fountain   232
What of the darkness? Is it very fair?   117
What spirit do I house?   148
"What time is it?" said the one,   207
What years of slow erosion, tide and ice   82
When a gull falls   135
When bombs on Barcelona burst,   72
When he went blundering back to God,   215
When I am dead and sister to the dust;   6
When I am ended, and I see no more   58
When, in the gold October dusk, I saw you near to setting,   210
When my time came   4
When the aster's smoke-blue   10
When the Norn Mother saw the Whirlwind Hour   141
Where Sanderlings, like children, run   100
Whether at noon or dawn this ship was steered   145
White sky, over the hemlocks bowed with snow,   152
Who is weeping in the apartment above?   203
Within an orbit of aloofness, each   66
Within the mirror of an oval dream   162
Word of her plight is on the wing,   172

Y

You came once through the blue dusk of the evening   120
Your blood runs muddled,   111